AUBREY COHEN COLLEGE LIBRARY
75 Varick St. 12th Floor
New York, NY 10013

A SYSTEMS CHANGE APPROACH TO SUBSTANCE ABUSE PREVENTION

A SYSTEMS CHANGE APPROACH
TO SUBSTANCE ABUSE PREVENTION

Edited by

Jacob U. Gordon

Studies in Health and Human Services
Volume 26

Library of Congress Cataloging-in-Publication Data

A systems change approach to substance abuse prevention / edited by Jacob U. Gordon.
    p. cm. -- (Studies in health and human services ; v. 26)
    Includes bibliographical references and index.
    ISBN 0-7734-8781-6
    1. Drug abuse--United States--Prevention. 2. Drug abuse--Prevention--Study and teaching--United States. 3. Social work with narcotic addicts--United States. I. Gordon, Jacob U. II. Series.
HV5825.S946 1997
362.29'17'0973--dc21
                                                                         96-39801
                                                                             CIP

This is volume 26 in the continuing series
Studies in Health and Human Services
Volume 26 ISBN 0-7734-8781-6
SHHS Series ISBN 0-88946-126-0

A CIP catalog record for this book is available from the British Library.

Copyright © 1997 The Edwin Mellen Press

All rights reserved. For information contact

    The Edwin Mellen Press   The Edwin Mellen Press
    Box 450   Box 67
    Lewiston, New York   Queenston, Ontario
    USA 14092-0450   CANADA L0S 1L0

                  The Edwin Mellen Press, Ltd.
                  Lampeter, Ceredigion, Wales
                UNITED KINGDOM SA48 8LT

                Printed in the United States of America

Dedication

To Project Neighboorhood and
all the advocates for systems change.

Acknowledgements

The publication of this volume is made possible by Fighting Back (Project Neighborhood) and the Jackson County anti-drug tax in Kansas City, Missouri.

The editor would like to express appreciation to his program assistant, Bridgitt Hardin; Mary Brohammer for typing and Katie Woods, my research assistant, for proofreading the manuscript; and the staff of Project Neighborhood, especially Gwendolyn Turner and David York, for their timeless efforts in organizing the symposium which produced the scholarly papers included in this book. I am also grateful to my contributors and Andy Spickard, M.D., the national director of Fighting Back for helping me to define the choice framework and clarify the purpose of the manuscript. Once again, thanks to my wife, Thelma, and family for their encouragement and support.

Table of Contents

Acknowledgements vi

Foreword
   Anderson Spickard, Jr., M.D. ix

Introduction
   Jacob U. Gordon xiii

1   A Systemic Analysis of Substance Abuse Prevention:
    Vision, Polemics, and Hope
       Omowale Amuleru-Marshall 1

2   School-Based Adolescent Drug Prevention:
    What Works and What Doesn't Work, What's Next?
       Nancy S. Tobler 21

3   Substance Abuse, Violence, and Crime
       Alberto G. Mata, Jr. 33

4   Health Promotion: Strategies for a Generation at Risk
       Richard P. Keeling, M.D., and Eric L. Engstrom 47

5   Developing an Infrastructure for Community Prevention
       Darlind J. Davis and Michael R.J. Felix 55

6 Ethnographic Research Methods for Multicultural Community
   Needs Assessment: A Systems Change Perspective
   Kristi O'Dell and Edith M. Freeman   75

7 Fighting Back (Project Neighborhood) and Systems Change
   Keith Brown   99

8 Community Exchange: An Imperative in
   Substance Abuse Policy Development
   Tamara J. Cadet 123

9 Recommendations
   • Prevention Infrastructure
       James Copple 139
   • Prevention Networks
       Edith M. Freeman 141
   • Systemic Support
       Janine Lee 142
   • Research and Evaluation
       Mary Jo Larson 143

10 Where Do We Go From Here?
   Jacob U. Gordon 147

Bibliography 155

Appendices 177

Author Index 187

Subject Index 189

Contributors 195

Foreword

•The devastation caused by illegal drugs, alcohol, and tobacco in individuals, families, and communities is a modern day plague in America at the close of the Twentieth Century. The problems posed by substance abuse are so complex that exceptionally well-coordinated strategies are required to deal with the many aspects of prevention, treatment, and after-care for people most affected by substance abuse.• Our schools use precious time and resources to attempt to prevent initial drug use. Our treatment centers are overwhelmed with waiting lists of people needing help and our neighborhoods are attempting to cope with a wide range of visible and invisible damage resulting from each new wave of the epidemic. How long must we endure the pain, the lost years of human life, the drain on our resources and on our spirits?

•Those of us who pay attention full-time to the insidious toll taken by substance abuse know this—the use and abuse of illegal drugs, alcohol, and tobacco has become normal behavior for large numbers of Americans from every social class, from every ethnic group, in every community across our country. We simply take for granted that a long holiday weekend will see as many lives lost to the effects of substance abuse as would be lost in the collision of two jumbo jets full of people. However, there will be no special investigation—simply a grim tally duly reporting the numbers dead in car crashes and shootings.•

There is no simple panacea to get us out of the crisis we find ourselves in. We cannot simply delegate the problem to the police, to the treatment providers, to the political leadership, to the courts, or to any other conceivable group to whom we often turn for expert help. The problems require the most difficult kind of response—a widespread concentration of our hearts, minds, and money to change the community norms that encourage substance abuse and to change the individual behavior that so casually spreads the epidemic from person to person, from generation to generation.

The encouraging news is that, since about 1989, there has been an exponential growth of new kinds of community level; collaboration attempting to design more powerful, community-wide strategies to go after this terrible plague on the local level. In late 1989 and throughout 1990 both the Robert Wood Johnson Foundation and the federal government's Center for Substance Abuse Prevention began to award grants to communities who participated in extensive competitive application processes. Hundreds of other communities got no outside help but have moved ahead anyway. In the ensuing years, we have learned that community leaders and ordinary citizens alike were eager to take on the challenge. We learned that every type of community—from rural New Mexico, to inner-city Kansas City, to wealthy Santa Barbara were struggling with variations of the same issues. We have seen that honorable people often disagree about the particular solutions proposed for substance abuse problems but they see and feel a sense of urgency to respond more assertively as the plague inexorably and predictably takes many lives, damages many more, and leaves neighborhoods with numerous visible reminders that the infection continues to rage.

Are we beginning to make headway in our fight against substance abuse? Can we find ways to "hate the addiction but love the addict" as Father George Clements teaches us? Have any communities learned to provide the protection to poorer young people that are often enjoyed by richer people? Are we finding ways to arouse the citizenry to compassionate action and avoid the trap of vigilantism? Do we know any more about the constellation of qualities needed to make a community more drug resistant? Do we have models that demonstrate, low-cost, community-based living arrangements for those struggling with a long recovery process from a disease that is both chronic and recurring? Have we learned how to assess particular substance abuse problems and calculate their costs so that elected officials can get a better grip on the future resources and policies that have highest potential? Have we learned how to engage young people themselves in designing more nurturing communities with appropriate safety nets for those whose home lives are less than optimal? The answer to all of these questions is a resounding YES!

No community has done all of these things but all of these things have been achieved in some communities.

It is time to learn from each other; to adopt and adapt successful approaches from other communities in our communities; it is time to apply what we are learning to achieve in each community what some call the "threshold effect," the "critical mass," or the "tipping point" so that the curve of our terrible epidemic begins as a descent as rapid as its rise. With this volume, Professor Jacob U. Gordon is providing us with some of the literature we need to assist in this process. There is more to learn, more to share, and more challenges than we care to think about at one time. The most dangerous terrorist threat of our time is not the anonymous bomber; it is the complacent indifference of ordinary citizens to the diminished quality of life caused by substance abuse in every community in America.

> Anderson Spickard, Jr., M.D., Professor
> Vanderbilt University Medical Center
> and Director, Fighting Back National Program Office

Introduction

This book is a product of a symposium on substance abuse organized by Project Neighborhood, Inc., in Kansas City, Missouri, November 30-December 2, 1995. Project Neighborhood (PNH) is one of fourteen National Fighting Back Initiatives funded by the Robert Wood Johnson Foundation. Its primary goal is the reduction of alcohol and illicit drugs. The purpose of the symposium in Kansas City was to create a collective vision for Kansas City as a community with regards to substance abuse prevention and technical assistance. The symposium was used as a vehicle for impacting systems change by creating prevention resource systems for the community.

This book explores some of the guiding principles, core structural components, operational functions of prevention resource system framework and the functional areas with a community prevention training system. It presents some of the relevant papers at the symposium and summarizes ideas and strategies that were subjects of discussion at the symposium's major workshops.

For years professionals, policymakers, practitioners, and customers have talked about the impact of substance abuse on the American society. The plight of America's cities—how these cities have deteriorated; how they have become centers of crime with poor housing, poor schools, and poor economic infrastructure, have been traditionally focused on individuals needing services.

Several cases in point are welfare services, mental health, substance abuse prevention and treatment, education, economic development, and prison rehabilitation services. Very little emphasis, if any, has been placed on systems change. The term "systems change" means that the current ineffective human service delivery policies and practices are outcome based. It means more investment of American resources in what works, as scientifically determined—scientific outcome based evaluation. For human service providers, systems change is a change in paradigm—in the way human service businesses are being conducted. The knowledge of what works and what doesn't work is there, but it appears that America lacks the political will to impact systems change. It has been estimated that the cost to American taxpayers is about $350 billion per year. This cost will be substantially reduced if America stops investing in what doesn't work.

A generation ago, following the burning of a number of America's cities in the riots of the late 1960s, the Kerner Commission issued a report detailing the degradation of life in the inner cities and provided numerous recommendations on how conditions could be improved. In 1993 the Milton S. Eisenhower Foundation (Curtis, 1995) issued a follow-up report showing that little, if anything, had been accomplished since 1969. In fact, the Eisenhower report indicated that conditions were worse than ever before. Today, according to the report, as middle-class Americans of all races continue to flee to the suburbs and exurbs and many lower-skilled manufacturing jobs are being moved overseas, America is faced with the enormous job of not only physically rebuilding the cities, but of rebuilding their economic structures and living environments as well. The inner core of urban areas and large cities have become balkanized, neglected outposts of deterioration, joblessness, substance abuse, teenage parenthood, crimes and self-destructive behaviors. Families now earn less than they did 30 years ago. Fifty percent of African-American children and 40 percent of Hispanic children younger than six years of age live in poverty.

The Joint Center for Political and Economic Studies reports that urban areas are home to 75 percent of African-Americans, 60 percent of Native Americans, and 95 percent of immigrants of color. Between 1980 and 1990 roughly 40 percent of population growth in the United States resulted from immigration. Seventy-five percent of those immigrants were either Latino or Asian, and 95 percent of those immigrants have settled in and around the ten largest American cities—where African-Americans and American Indians already live. In addition to this demographic change, the Kerner report and the implementation of its recommendations have failed to ameliorate conditions. For example,

Introduction xv

racism is still very much alive. In fact, America has moved from two societies (one black, one white—and unequal) to three societies—black, white, and Hispanic. In 1963, the unemployment rate for African-Americans was 10.8 percent; it is now more than 14 percent. And yet America has pumped billions of dollars into the Great Society Project, the anti-poverty war and the war against drugs.

In the face of these alarming trends and disheartening conditions, the author is pleased to offer this volume as a framework for outcome based systems change. In the following ten chapters, the contributors to this volume have developed new approaches to old and familiar issues in the substance abuse field.

Omowale Amuleru-Marshall presents a systemic analysis of substance abuse prevention. Using the public health model, Dr. Amuleru-Marshall has advocated a shift in emphasis from interventions that are directed at individuals to those that are directed at systems and ecology.

The second chapter by Nancy Tobler documents the effectiveness of school-based drug prevention programs. This chapter highlights the successful approaches that are not in marketable form that can be placed in the hands of teachers or principals. Nancy also identifies the types of programs that don't work. This raises the question: Why are we still using those approaches that are not working? She proposes the replication of what works and abandoning what doesn't work.

The third chapter successfully documents the obvious but often neglected relationship between substance abuse and violence and crime in America. Professor Alberto Mata provides alarming data on the extent to which substance abuse directly and/or indirectly affects the increase of violence and crimes in American society. He argues that if violence and crimes are to be reduced in America, substance abuse must be prevented, particularly among the youth.

In agreeing with Professor Mata, Eric Engstrom and Richard Keeling, M.D., have developed new health promotion strategies for a generation at risk. They see this approach as a new agenda for health promotion in the 1990s and the 21st century. The new agenda includes a global perspective about the challenges that have created so many changes for this generation at risk; recognizing the roots of these problems in American culture; acting locally and with vision and decisiveness to build skills, nurture, and heal self-esteem; providing strong support and involvement in connecting communities as caring networks of concerned people.

The fifth chapter examines the partnerships among public, private, and philanthropic organizations and their relationship in building an infrastructure to solve substance abuse problems. Darlind Davis and Michael Felix have articulated the challenges facing the nation's capacity to solve complicated health and human service issues, especially when viewed in the context of budget deficits, health care reform, lack of national uniform policy for local-based constituency building, lack of coordination among funders, competition among service providers, and a lack of ownership for issues by local citizens. Among other things, Davis and Felix have recommended that a more formalized national/public/private/philanthropic partnership be supported with mandates to plan, implement, and support local-based constituency building groups toward a healthy America.

The sixth chapter focuses on the impact of ethnographic research methods on multicultural community-based systems. Ms. Kristi O'Dell, a doctoral candidate, and her advisor Professor Edith Freeman at the University of Kansas School of Social Welfare, have examined the use of ethnographic research methods in conducting community needs assessment. They agree that baseline data collection and the identification of existing community strengths and weaknesses are prerequisites to systems change.

Chapter seven discusses what works in the substance abuse field. Keith Brown, the executive director of Kansas City Fighting Back (Project Neighborhood) highlights five programmatic areas of success: public awareness, prevention in the faith community—Project Save, community mobilization models, alcohol public policy-covenants with liquor store owners, and treatment referral and tracking systems. As one of the fourteen national demonstration substance abuse reduction projects funded by the Robert Wood Johnson Foundation, Project Neighborhood has successfully documented what works in a community-based substance abuse program.

Tamara Cadet of Join Together provides a much needed perspective in the substance abuse field. She examines the concept and practice of "community exchange" as an imperative in shaping public policy issues in substance abuse. Among other things, she points out the significance of public policy agenda as the driving force in alcohol, tobacco, and other drug (ATOD) prevention, intervention, and treatment. The development of national and local drug policies must be inclusive. In this context, community exchange is a necessary vehicle for mobilizing citizens to share ideas and develop strategies to impact public policy. This eighth chapter focuses on the main thrust of this volume—systems change through community empowerment to impact ATOD policy.

Chapter nine summarizes the position papers and recommendations of four workshops which focused on key structural components of prevention resource systems: prevention infrastructure, prevention networks, systemic support, and research and evaluation. Two academics, Professor Edith Freeman of the University of Kansas and Dr. Mary Jo Larson of Brandeis University provide summaries on prevention networks and research evaluation, respectively. Janine Lee, a senior foundation officer, developed the systemic support paper. James Copple, a national expert on coalition building, guides the report on prevention infrastructure.

The final chapter by Jacob Gordon, editor of this volume, addresses two critical questions: Where do we go from here? Can the American prevention community afford to remain fragmented, or will it work together as a well-coordinated and caring community? His response to the second is emphatically no to the status quo. Drawing on his experiences as an academic, practitioner, and advocate of systems change, Professor Gordon provides a framework on where the prevention community must go from here. He urges the prevention and treatment communities and policymakers to invest more in what works and replicate those things rather than reinventing the wheel.

1

A Systemic Analysis of Substance Abuse Prevention: Vision, Polemics, and Hope

Omowale Amuleru-Marshall, Ph.D. M.P.H.

This discussion begins with a review of the prevention paradigm inherent in public health practice. In this context, it attempts an advocacy for a shift in emphasis from interventions that are directed at individuals to those that are directed at systems, indeed at the ecology in which individuals are sequestered. The environment in which most African Americans are forced to exist is considered as some fundamental elements of a just social order. This brings into sharp focus the nature of the individual/institution interface and the marginalization of the African American community. The effort to expand health and well-being among African Americans is unequivocally presented as one that targets the dismantling of inequitable social arrangements which breed domination and exclusion.

The Prevention Paradigm

⁕Prevention activities can target any aspect of the entire drug market spectrum. Starting with the cultivation or processing of the raw materials, prevention activities may be directed at the source of the mood-altering substances. They may be directed to the methods and vehicles of transportation or at the wholesale and retail distribution of these substances. All of these targets of prevention are actually more critical than the single dimension of consumption. Yet even at the level of consumption, there are a number of different possible targets for prevention.⁕

Targets for prevention are traditionally categorized according to whether they are resident in the *environment* in which the problem is found, or in the *agent* or disease-bearing vector, or in the *host* or victim of the problem (Taylor, et al., 1982). The boundaries between these categories are often fused and intervention targets can sometimes be multi-dimensional (Amuleru-Marshall, 1993). Etiological processes or causative factors are, therefore, not always clear or easily accessible to intervention. However, when interventions are mounted, they are conceptually driven by the conventional prevention paradigm in public health practice. It posits a continuum from primary, through secondary, to tertiary prevention (Last, 1986; 1992). Working in reverse order, these dimensions will now be discussed as they relate to substance abuse prevention.

Tertiary Prevention

Tertiary prevention is directed at the hosts or victims of drug abuse and addiction and is interchangeable with the practices recognized as treatment (Johnson, 1986). That treatment services are simultaneously preventive services has been a problematic percept for those with a tendency to think dichotomously. Many people in the substance abuse field juxtapose prevention against treatment as if they were mutually exclusive sets of activities (Edwards, et al., 1994).

Tertiary prevention in the substance abuse field refers to detoxification, chemically assisted or drug-free treatment, and relapse prevention. Detoxification can be either on an inpatient or outpatient, ambulatory basis and has traditionally been medically managed, frequently with the use of pharmacotherapy. There has been the more recent emergence of *social* detoxification services; places where drug-addicted persons can be withdrawn from the chemicals to which they have become dependent without the use of other chemicals. Treatment can be of various intensities and durations, and it can be provided on an outpatient, inpatient, or long-term residential basis. Finally, relapse prevention services include halfway or threequarterway houses, aftercare programs and self-help, support groups such as Alcoholics Anonymous (AA), Narcotics Anonymous (NA), Cocaine Anonymous (CA), and Methadone Anonymous (MA). The notion of relapse prevention illustrates why treatment can also be thought of as prevention. This last stage of *treatment* is designed to *prevent* a return to the active disease course of addiction. Only 20 percent of treated clients remain drug-free for one year after treatment.

Approximately two-thirds relapse by three-months follow-up (Catalano, et al., 1988; Groves and Amuleru-Marshall, 1994). Even the much-vaunted, 12-step, self-help programs experience significant rates of failure. It typically takes several treatment attempts before a drug addicted person successfully recovers the sobriety or chemical health that drug abuse compromises.

Treatment, then, is an attempt to *prevent* the further decompensation of the drug-abusing or drug-addicted client who struggles with compulsivity, denial, confusion, narcissism, dishonesty, scarcity obsessions, control illusions, affective alienations, pain phobias and ethical/spiritual crises. It requires a knowledge of substance abuse epidemiology including known risk factors such as familial risk patterns and dynamics. Drug procurement and use practices in the local area as well as clinical presentations and diagnostic criteria for intoxication, abuse, and dependence must also be known. The health consequences, drug interactions, and ethical/legal issues associated with commonly abused drugs as well as the conventional ways in which treatment is provided are fundamental to an addiction therapist's fund of knowledge. This knowledge base is supported by a repertoire of professional skills such as drug use history taking and clinical assessment, including the appropriate use of available screening instruments. Treatment planning, referring, and case management join counseling, clinical prevention, and charting to define a basic catalogue of skills to support tertiary prevention or treatment activities (Task Force on Alcohol and Drugs, 1987). It must be pointed out that the effective prevention of substance abuse cannot occur until competent, confidential, financially, and culturally accessible treatment services are available to all drug addicted persons on demand.

Secondary Prevention

Secondary prevention is considered to be appropriate in cases of early onset of a disease or where especially high risk conditions differentiate particular persons from the general at-risk population. Obviously, it is always better to find cases earlier than later. As was suggested during the discussion of treatment, when the condition of chemical dependency is allowed to develop to an advanced stage, the prognosis in most cases is quite bleak. Secondary prevention, then, concerned as it is with early diagnosis and prevention, is dedicated to outreach, screening, referral, or intervention (Johnson, 1986; Amuleru-Marshall, 1990).

Screening and intervention activities can be mounted in a variety of settings (Last, 1992). Community-based information and referral services, hotlines and crisis centers, student assistance and employee assistance programs, primary health clinics, and social service agencies are examples of professional settings where screening does or can occur. Screening activities can also be set up in police stations, courts, and emergency rooms where drug-related arrests and emergencies can be monitored (Edwards, et al., 1994). Finally, churches, lodges, sororities, fraternities, and social clubs are some of the non-professional organizations through which screening can occur. Special initiatives such as health fairs and screening booths at malls, grocery stores, and airports offer additional case-finding opportunities.

Some of the special high-risk conditions that have been associated with drug use include sensation-seeking and risk-taking lifestyles, rebellious and normless tendencies, and a high tolerance for deviance. A sense of alienation from the community, school, church, or from one's family has also been associated with substance abuse risk (CSAP, 1993). Certainly, a limited perception of risk coupled with an exaggerated perception of popular use increases one's risk to drug abuse as does early drug use initiation, early anti-social behavior, *ahistoricity*, and *purposelessness*. Shyness and social reticence can also lead to self-medication. It can also be said that the more independence, deviance, alienation, rebelliousness, adventurism, apathy, and distress and the less achievement, religiosity, and conformity, the more the risk increases (Hawkins, et al., 1990; CSAP, 1993).

Family characteristics such as family drug abuse, disorganized and normless family relations, parental pampering, and indulgence or abuse and neglect have all been promulgated to increase risk (Alvy, 1991). Interventions designed to address populations with special risks or with early onset of substance abuse must be more textured than those prepared for primary prevention. However, they would not be as intensive as those designed for treatment. Besides, to treat persons for whom secondary prevention is appropriate in settings that are designed for drug-addicted clients might have counterproductive consequences, such as the cultivation of denial and minimization or other poor outcomes. Psycho-educational and counseling interventions especially designed to correct special vulnerabilities or extinguish drug-using behavior can be mounted through university counseling services or other school-based, worksite-based, or community-based projects and agencies.

Primary Prevention

Primary prevention is appropriate in all situations in which the targeted persons are healthy with respect to the problem being prevented although they may belong to groups that are characterized by excessive prevalence of the disease in focus. Its purpose is to inoculate persons and groups by decreasing their known risk factors and/or increasing their known resiliency factors. Primary prevention of substance abuse typically is thought to include public awareness, public education, attitude and behavior change or reinforcement, and social or public action.

It incorporates public awareness strategies such as public service announcements, advertisements, press conferences, press materials, and public fora. Public education requires more in-depth coverage on TV, radio, or in newspaper features. It may involve parental mobilization and education, or symposia for key influencers, and typically employs topical curricula and other health education materials. Examples of the kind of information that might be transmitted are epidemiological distributions, availability sources, laws and regulatory practices, negative consequences of use, inoculation strategies, risk and resiliency factors. The intended impact of public awareness or public education is on individuals; they are, therefore, host-anchored strategies.

While attitude and behavior change represent more challenging outcomes of primary prevention, they are also host-anchored strategies. Typically, prevention initiatives to change attitudes and behavior can include health promotion curricula and other strategies in organized interventions, training programs for professionals, peer leaders, and volunteers, or the establishment of a national and regional training and technical assistance capacity to support local efforts. Interventions to change attitudes and behaviors are targeted to specific outcomes such as increasing resistance strategies, problem-solving, decision-making, impulse-control, coping behaviors, social competency, academic skills, or parenting efficacy. These interventions are often strengthened by the inclusion of activities which represent alternatives to drug abuse or which facilitate cultural transformation.

It is difficult to become actively committed to activities such as neighborhood clean-up, security for elders, academic and athletic coaching, sports and other physically challenging activities, photography, art, or drama and, at the same time, pursue the escalating consumption of mind-altering drugs. Similarly, the transformative exploration of the history, political experience, folklore, and customs of one's ethnic group militates against involvement in practices which threaten that group's well being.

Social/public action is the approach to primary prevention which takes attention away from the *host* and places as the central target of interventions the *agent* and the *environment* (McLeroy, et al., 1993). Interventions directed at the agent—the drugs themselves—may target, as noted before, the cultivation and processing of raw materials. They may be directed at the methods and vehicles of transporting, wholesaling, or retailing these chemical agents, illegal and legal. Therefore, such issues as drug-free zones, police patrols, and protection join those of availability and licensure, price and taxation, regulation and enforcement, advertisement and promotions controls as targets. A community organized to protest against excessive alcohol/tobacco advertising or inappropriate marketing in places frequented by children and youth is an example of social or public policy prevention.

Communities may be organized and mobilized, as a strategy of substance abuse prevention, to effect greater empowerment, neighborhood improvement, school renovation and reform, job creation, the provision of facilities and opportunities for cultural and recreational activities, or legislative and judicial initiatives for socioeconomic and political change. The point is that direct political action for social change targeting improvements in education, housing, employment, healthcare, and community empowerment are no less legitimate and likely, more effective, strategies of substance abuse prevention than host-anchored interventions. There is ample evidence that socioeconomically underdeveloped communities in general, and particularly those that are also outside of the Eurocentric cultural mainstream, are veritable repositories of substance abuse risk and prevalence (Amuleru-Marshall, in press).

The use of the mass media in substance abuse prevention should not be limited to increasing individuals' awareness and changing their behavior. Unfortunately, the influence of social marketing in disease prevention and health promotion has tended to limit the employment of the media to efforts targeted at individual behavior. Social marketing, derived from the discipline of marketing, is viewed as a structured process, an exchange that is consumer/user oriented. It deals with audience segments in a mix of controllable variables such as price, promotion, product, and place (NCI, 1989; Maibach, et al., 1993). The mass media can, in fact, be used to support a variety of activities across all the primary preventive dimensions. For example, the media can be used, as stated earlier, to create awareness, provide information, demonstrate skills, and reinforce healthy behaviors. They can also be used to set agenda, establish credibility, and support other communication channels, projects, and mobilizations.

Various mass media channels are available and can be employed singly or in combination, depending on resources, media advocacy skills, and opportunities. There are channels which derive from the medium of television such as feature programs, public service announcements, and news. There are newspaper-based channels such as articles, letters, editorials, and calendars as well as magazine-based examples such as features, news, events, and calendars. Other miscellaneous channels include booklets, flyers, posters, stickers, and other print materials. Additionally, special newsletters can be used to provide news, updates, and features. Finally, cyberspace channels can be expected to become increasingly available in the future.

Etiology

In order to attempt to prevent substance abuse, some consideration must be given to particular causes of these problems. One's understanding of cause-effect relationships provides the logic for prevention interventions. While possibly confusing, it has been recommended that causes may also be understood as primary, secondary, or tertiary (Amuleru-Marshall, in press). This perspective invites an understanding of substance abuse etiology which is multi-factorial, multi-generational, and interactive (Abbey, et al., 1993). It resists precise, linear, cause-effect models and favors a willingness to view some causes as effects, themselves (Cooper, et al., 1994). A useful analogy to enlighten this etiological perspective could be a tree with its *roots* representing primary causes or historical and sociostructural factors. These then give rise to *trunk* or secondary causes composed of micro-ecological factors. These, in turn, condition the development of *branch* or tertiary causes which are familial and person-specific factors. While consistent with the traditional public health practice of identifying causes in the environment, in the disease-bearing vector or agent, as well as in the host, this approach places the ultimate culpability in the environment. To limit one's attention and interventions to the tertiary and secondary dimensions with individuals and their immediate families, however successful one's efforts are, is to co-exist, and tacitly collaborate, with the very conditions that cause the malformations that one is attempting to remediate (Amuleru-Marshall, in press).

The plethora of activities that a comprehensive substance abuse prevention agenda would require begs the question of whether the United States of America, in its vast national breadth and wealth, values a drug-free society enough to sponsor it. Especially in today's political climate, driven as it is by Republican ideas of social Darwinism and economic eugenics, there is a strengthened unwillingness in the body politic to assume financial responsibility for the inoculation of whole communities or even persons. As inadequate as their funded initiatives were, the federal agencies charged with supporting substance abuse prevention and treatment find themselves in a climate in which their resources are threatened with significant reductions and dispersions. A return to the politics of states' rights portends that particular groups in this country, most notably those who are historically oppressed, will experience a tightening of the links of the chains of oppression in many localities.

Community Reconsidered

Attempts to clearly define the elusive concept of community can be traced to the community mental health movement of the 1960s (Biddle and Biddle, 1965; Akbar, et al., 1980). The term community has been used to describe a wide variety of human aggregations. Some published definitions of community have tended to be structural, referring to such entities as a neighborhood, an entire city, or a metropolitan complex. The term has also been given functional definitions based upon the citizens' awareness of community (Biddle and Biddle, 1965).

The following two definitions of community would seem to exemplify both of these approaches: (1) A social group of any size whose members reside in a specific locality, share government, and have a common cultural and historical heritage. (2) A social group sharing common characteristics or interests and perceived or perceiving itself as distinct in some respect from the larger society in which it exists (Mann, 1978). The latter definition permits such uses as the frequent designation of a national black *community* or local black *communities* which transcend geographic boundaries. Since the term is also frequently used to designate geographic areas such as particular neighborhoods, the following exception may need to be entertained. When members of historically underdeveloped or oppressed groups, such as African Americans, reside in predominantly white neighborhoods, the attribution of community should probably not be made because the residents do not share a common cultural and historical heritage.

It is precisely in the areas of cultural and historical heritage that black and white Americans differ most. Many African American scholars, analysts, and commentators have argued that the fundamental crisis confronting the African in America is that of cultural domination (Karenga, 1989; Nobles, 1985). The result is an abiding inability to resolve the problem of cultural identity and to answer accurately as a group the question, *who are we?* This contemporary crisis has its origins in the historical heritage of the *maafa*—the holocaust of chattel slavery. We cannot begin to understand and consequently address the myriad social problems and epidemics which confront black communities across this country if we do not return to this corridor of atrocities in which our transformation to the community of excessive mortality, excessive morbidity, and excessive incarceration began (Amuleru-Marshall, 1992).

Indices of Social Inequity

Bulhan (1985), suggested that these three indices—excessive mortality, excessive morbidity, and excessive incarceration—provide the most visible signs of endemic social inequity. This society's endemic inequity expresses itself as sociostructural racism. Sociostructural racism is the most lethal form of racism, from which the other three types—institutional, interpersonal, and intrapersonal racism—derive. It gives the overwhelming impression of representing the *natural order of things,* and is, therefore, the least discernible type of racism. It pervades the prevailing values, social relations, the entire environment, indeed, even individual psyches. Its impact is to impose the greatest hardships on the largest number of persons in the affected groups and it is a major contributor to premature deaths (Bulhan, 1985). Sociostructural racism has been defined as the historical and systematic arrangement of productive and social relations so that they, without extraordinary intervention, develop a certain racial group and, dialectically, underdevelop other racial groups (Amuleru-Marshall, 1992; 1993).

Ahistorical and superficial attempts to amalgamate communities without regard for history, class, and culture are harnessed by the perplexing consistency of certain patterns of underdevelopment and oppression which transcend localities, municipalities, metropolitan boundaries, and even regions. They salute the notions of a national black community and of a disenfranchised national colony. When death rates from the fifteen leading causes are compared between black and white Americans, black men are found to have the highest rate for each major cause, except diabetes mellitus, chronic obstructive pulmonary diseases and suicide, and for all causes combined. Black women have the highest mortality rates for diabetes mellitus and white men die more as a result of the other two causes. In fact, black males' combined death rates for all causes, the highest rate of excessive mortality of any race/sex group in the United States, is 1.7 times greater than the next highest combined death rate (white males), while black females' combined death rate from all causes is 1.6 times greater than the next highest female rate (white females). In particular cases such as homicide and AIDS, the differentials between black and white persons are so large that they demand analysis of the sociostructural context in which these problems emerge (National Center for Health Statistics (NCHS), 1990).

Indices of morbidity such as *limitation of activity caused by chronic conditions,* and *respondent assessed health status,* conform to the established pattern of excessive black health problems. Of course, black men and women have the highest rates of hypertension and obesity, respectively, in comparison with each other and with white men and women (NCHS, 1990).

In the United States, there are at least thirty states where the black prisoners constitute 25 to 95 percent of the total prison population, yet there are only seven states and the District of Columbia where black citizens represent 20 percent or more of the total population. In 1991, black men, who constitute only about 5.9 percent of the nation's population, represented 45.5 percent of male state prison inmates. Black women, 6.5 percent of the national population, represented 46 percent of female state prison inmates. In the federal system, African Americans contributed 33.8 percent of prisoners in 1993 (Maguire and Pastore, 1994).

Most Americans of African ancestry live their lives in what has been called the *mundane extreme environment.* These environments, which are viewed as the products of sociostructural racism, are characterized by poverty in a society with a materialistic ethos, by unemployment and underemployment, by maleducation and miseducation, by dense clustering of individuals in inadequate housing, by inadequate and unavailable health care, by disempowerment and dependency, and by environmental pollutants, including the relatively excessive availability of alcohol, tobacco, and other drugs (Pierce, 1970). Clearly, substance abuse among African Americans is symptomatic of a larger societal dilemma which threatens the entire community's right to thrive.

The Social Justice Imperative of Public Health

Under desirable sociopolitical and cultural circumstances, individuals should enjoy a reciprocally-deterministic relationship with their environments. This is another way of stating that they and the groups they represent should be fully enfranchised so that they can contribute to the evolving transformations of the structures and institutions which, in turn, shape their humanity. Under these circumstances, the following truths become self-evident: "That all [persons] . . . are created equal; that they are endowed by their Creator with certain unalienable rights; that among these are life, liberty, and the pursuit of happiness" (Continental Congress, 1776).

The ideas that follow draw heavily from a work by the Honorable Michael Manley, former Prime Minister of Jamaica (1974). Any society that strives to be just must pursue the objectives of self-reliance, equality, and democracy. Any sociopolitical system which professes a moral purpose must be concerned with social justice. This is the conscious effort to regulate the relations between all members of a society in a manner that is predictable and capable of rational exposition, and that takes into account the proportional weight of each group's claim upon the total society. Social justice cannot exist where decisions are arbitrary and unpredictable. Social justice requires that dynamic changes must be acceptable to all of the people. Finally, social justice posits that egalitarianism is the only enduring moral basis for social organization.

This notion is fundamentally important to the prevention of substance abuse or the building of a healthy society in that it reflects an intersect of purpose with that of social/public policy prevention. Wallack and colleagues (1993) make the case in the following way:

> Social justice principles assume that as citizens, people share responsibility for the conditions in society as well as a strong obligation to the collective good. In practice, this means that we are obliged to hold ourselves as well as our social institutions responsible for ensuring the conditions in which all members of the community can be healthy. Social

justice steers us away from a narrow concern over the health of individuals toward the health of the population at large. Individual well-being depends on community well-being. This means that health is a political endeavour as much as, or at times even more than, a medical one. It means that how we operate as a society and who has a voice in decision-making are public health concerns. . . . While market justice perspectives legitimize and emphasize traditional (usually reductionistic) medical and technical approaches, social justice perspectives broaden the focus to include the social and political arena (p. 15).

Elements of a Just Social Order

If social justice is fundamental to public health, it is a prerequisite for a drug free society. What then are the basic elements of a just social order? Michael Manley (1974) elaborates the following four categories: The first category is a material one which incorporates three fundamental needs. A just society should so organize itself that every willing and able citizen is provided with an opportunity to work. When this opportunity does not exist, all other human rights take on the quality of fantasy. Secondly, there are the three basic essentials of civilized existence: food, shelter and clothing. Finally, there are health care needs in their broadest understanding, incorporating health promotion and holistic health.

The second category of elements are psychocultural in nature incorporating three major elements. The first of these is the opportunity that each individual must have to participate in the political and economic decision-making of the society. The second element is a sense of belonging; a sense that the individual counts in the society. The third element is the opportunity for the creative use of leisure.

The third category is concerned with the rule of law in the society. The predictable and rational foundations of a just society must be enshrined in its system of laws. Its laws should ensure the appropriate checks and balances as well as basic protections which celebrate the humanity of each individual member of that society and, paradoxically, reduce each individual, irrespective of position or wealth, to the status of subject to this system of laws.

The final category concerns each individual's right to free, compulsory, universal education. There must be a realistic attempt to provide the expertise and skills that the society's developmental thrust requires and all citizens should have equal access, limited only by ability, to these training opportunities. This education, however, should not be limited to the transmission of formalized knowledge and technical skills. It must serve the more important function of teaching social responsibility, ethics, and culture. Culture, as a moral demand system, has the power to compel behavior and the capacity to reinforce ideas and beliefs about human activity. It represents the vast structure of behaviors, ideas, attitudes, values, habits, beliefs, customs, language, rituals, ceremonies, and practices of a particular group of people. A people's culture provides them with a general design for living and patterns for interpreting reality (Nobles and Goddard, 1993). This distinctive and complete design for living, while learned by direct and indirect observation, must also be taught quite explicitly (Landis, 1992). If there are different cultural groups in the society, this education, rather than homogenizing them, must grant to each group cultural self-confidence as they rediscover the cultural continuity to which they are heirs (Manley, 1974).

Endogenous and Exogenous Systems

A common way of distinguishing systems is by categorizing them as formal and informal organizations. Major conceptions advanced by classic organizational theorists, such as Max Weber (as cited in Blau and Scott, 1969), hold the characteristics of authority and bureaucracy to be fundamental to formal organizations. Other conceptions have included rational decision-making. While none of these traditional notions provide much assistance in honoring the distinction, formal organizations continue to be recognized in the contemporary period as those in which role expectations and behavior are explicitly established and regulated by the administrative apparatus. These organizations are characterized by extensive regulation and control of behavior. The term *informal* would usually be reserved for such organizations as churches, social clubs, and service clubs, because they are characterized by flexible structures and processes. Their tasks are not commonly governed by explicitly stated regulations and policies and employees are not strictly governed by a rigid, clearly specified authority structure (Bell, 1969). While of general interest, the distinction between formal and informal organizations is less useful to the purposes of this discussion than others that might be considered.

A more relevant distinction, for example, is between endogenous and exogenous organizations or agencies. This distinction is based on an analysis of who owns or controls an organization's functioning and who benefits from an organization's existence. Depending on an organization's goals and motives for existing, as well as clients served, its value system and cultural milieu will vary substantially. The term *exogenous systems* is being used to refer to those institutions and agencies that inhere in the public and private sectors of the mainstream American society. Conversely, the term *endogenous systems* is meant to refer to those institutions and agencies which inhere in a particular underdeveloped or ethnic community. The use of these terms is preferred so that the peripheral nature of the African American community's relationship to the mainstream is underlined.

Among the exogenous systems are governmental institutions, be they federal, state, county or municipal. Then there are private industrial and commercial, capital-formation enterprises—international, national, regional or local. There are also private not-for-profit agencies that might be international, national, regional or local. While many African Americans work in all three classes of exogenous systems, sometimes in quite senior positions, these systems are primarily neither committed to an African American agenda nor controlled by African American interests.

Exogenous organizations can be further classified according to their functions. For example, there are legislative and judicial institutions. There are military, police, prison and other security institutions. There are regulatory institutions, such as the FDA and the EPA. There are health services, educational, and social welfare institutions. There are labor relations, banking, manufacturing, service delivery, and information processing institutions. Mass media, arts, and entertainment institutions join with religious institutions to create a cultural superstructure. While this exemplary list is not exhaustive and contains a great deal of overlap, it does serve to illustrate the wide range of organizations that significantly impact our lives, despite our limited reciprocal influence.

When attention is turned to endogenous institutions or agencies, African Americans as a group will arguably be found to control no government institutions, except possibly for a few municipalities. African Americans control less than 1 percent of American industrial and commercial, capital-formation enterprises. African Americans, while more visible in the nonprofit sector, actually control a disproportionately small segment of the non-profit landscape as well. As a consequence, most of the African American person-institution interfaces that are fundamental to the maintenance of life in this society are with systems whose accountability, goals, motives, values, and cultural milieu are alien and alienating. They have evolved as institutions to serve the interests of the mainstream Eurocentric culture, and as such, imperceptibly maintain and perpetuate sociostructural racism.

This is why, even in the first year of life, African American infants, especially males, die at a rate that is virtually twice that of European American infants, a pattern of differential mortality which continues across our comparatively abbreviated lives. In fact, in particular localities, the black infant mortality and life expectancy rates are worse than the rates in many underdeveloped countries. This pattern of underdevelopment presents itself through a variety of indices beyond mortality, morbidity and incarceration, discussed above. Educational failure, expressed both by unparalleled dropout rates and miseducated successes, works in tandem with unparalleled unemployment rates. With a family structure that is crashing in unprecedented ways, the majority of black women and their children are left to struggle in desperation in institutionless, jobless, hopeless, crime-ridden neighborhoods. That this is the modal black experience cannot be equivocated despite the occasional flash of material success on the part of a few individuals and the molding of a buffer class of interlopers among the talented tenth.

> . . . whenever any form of [social organization] . . . becomes destructive to the ends of life, liberty and the pursuit of happiness, it is the right of the people to alter or to abolish it, and to institute new [arrangements] . . . laying [a] . . . foundation on such principles and organizing its powers in such form, as to them shall seem more likely to affect their Safety and Happiness. . . . When a long train of abuses and usurpations, pursuing invariably the same Object evinces a design to reduce them under absolute [racism] . . ., it is their right, it is their duty, to throw off such [social arrangements] . . . and to provide new guards for their future security (Continental Congress, 1776).

Rappaport (1977), drawing on the work of Ryan, suggested that in order to change social relationships, one must either change the powerful and powerless individuals themselves, or change the social structures that support their relationship. In essence, one is faced with a choice between working with individuals or with systems. In changing social systems, one will inevitably force change on both powerful and powerless individuals. The powerful will understandably resist such change, for it is clearly to their personal, economic, and social advantage to do so. This inevitably creates a conflict for many who hold powerful positions in our society, and who at the same time regard themselves as progressive, liberal, or non-racist.

> The way in which this conflict has been resolved by well meaning people who do not personally wish to hurt anyone, who are often personally appalled at racism and the results of poverty and powerlessness, but yet stand to lose a great deal of their own power and economic advantage should there be a massive redistribution of resources, is what William Ryan (1971) has termed 'blaming the victim.' . . . [Blaming the victim] involves a belief system, a way of viewing reality, and serves a function. Ryan argues that although it is not necessarily intentional, it serves the class interests of those who practice it. The norms of society are taken as a given, and deviation from those norms is a function of socialization. In Ryan's words, 'In defining social problems in this way the social pathologists are, of course, ignoring a whole set of factors that ordinarily might be considered relevant—for instance, unequal distribution of income, social stratification, political struggle, ethnic and racial group conflict, and inequality of power. Their ideology concentrates almost exclusively on the failure of the deviant. To the extent that society plays any part in social problems, it is said to have somehow failed to socialize the individual, to teach him how to adjust to circumstances, which, though far from perfect, are gradually changing for the better (p. 14).' . . . Victim blamers, argues Ryan, are all passing judgement on themselves and concluding that the problems are in the past inequities of society, they themselves are 'not guilty'. This enables one to 'help' the poor without threatening one's own privileged status. 'They will be entitled to what I have as soon as they are just like me' (Rappaport, 1977).

The alternatives for those who like the social system as it is, at least for themselves, while recognizing its consequences of poverty, inequality, disease and death, are both unacceptable extremes. As good, progressive, middle-class folk, they recognize that the view of social inequality as a necessary by-product of a basically good system is reactionary and repressive. On the other hand, to support radical sociostructural and economic change threatens their own class interests and well being (Rappaport, 1977). The dialectical relationship of development and underdevelopment imposes the reality that a more equitable distribution of income will necessarily mean less for those now in privileged or solidly middle-class positions. The resources in this society are not infinite. If the underprivileged and disempowered are to have more, the privileged and empowered will have to be content with less. In order for the black community to experience less unemployment, the white community will have to experience more unemployment. This inexorable seesaw of structural relationships is the liberal's dilemma.

Recommendations

The error of *preferred problem myopia* often precludes a consideration of certain solutions to the epidemic of substance abuse as it exacerbates the throes of chronic repression and underdevelopment which grips the African American community. Many professionals fail to recognize the usefulness of any discussion that does not present specific and immediate recommendations which permit them to tinker around the periphery of their preferred problem or specialty. However, if the reader followed the case presented here as it was developed up to this point, a single fact should be clear—*that substance abuse and addiction, with their chemical warfare implications and devastating sequelae in individuals, families and communities, are caused at the base by the historical processes of exclusion and domination.* An African proverb states that "if you do not know where you are going, any road will get you there." It is necessary to have a clear and unambivalent view of the ultimate goal of our efforts. If our work does not strive to expand, in its ultimate impact, the self-reliance, egalitarianism, as well as political and economic democracy for all groups of people in this society, we will exchange one social epidemic for another. We will burn out our liberal fervor and exhaust our professional lives in cyclical redundancies. We will not advance the public health without social justice. Therefore, the following recommendations seem reasonable:

In all of our efforts at prevention, we must seek to ensure that the authority, decision-making, and accountability are centered within the control of those most affected by the problem. We must seek to transform the submission to oppression which has been called *oppression illness* (Singer and Toledo as cited in Singer, 1995). Our efforts must reduce the dependence and apathy which are bred by domination and exclusion.

Transforming people from objects—mere props on the stage of history—to subjects of history is a health outcome worthy of our life's effort. Our individual projects should make sense as part of a much larger logic or social theory. In other words, their objectives should be very easily rationalized within this more comprehensive plan leading to the ultimate goals to which this work is dedicated. This recommendation requires that our individual services be coordinated by that logic and not operated at cross purposes, stricken by conflicts of turf, fiscal competition, and *scientific colonialism* (Nobles, 1985). Often we compartmentalize people, families, and communities according to our professional specialty, current job, department, funding source, and so forth, ignoring the comprehensive and complex nature of the assaults by which they are victimized.

Our efforts must rip away the mask of obscurity and shame from the face of our African heritage. They must result in the acquisition of cultural self-confidence and the rediscovery of the cultural continuity to which we are heirs (Manley, 1974). As Hilliard (1986), asserted, "No people can be liberated who are cultural neuters. Individuals may survive as shooting stars, with temporary spurts of speed, but with a curved path that ends in darkness. It is the group . . . that survives as an eternal galaxy."

Many people have suggested that the only effective way to guarantee the public health and well-being is to organize the community so that it can mobilize on its own behalf (Ryan as cited in Rappaport, 1977; Wallack, et al., 1993). Ryan (as cited in Rappaport, 1977) proposed, some time ago, the development of new mechanisms of government at the neighborhood level as well as ways in which professionals should conduct their interventions so that they do not function as what he called *the Giving Enemy*. These communities, in order to survive, must move from the politics of rights to the politics of power and resources.

A Systemic Analysis of Substance Abuse Prevention

The development of the capacity to be self-reliant will be ultimately based on the emergence of endogenous institutions and agencies. Their relative presence is a valid indicator of structural adjustments in the marginalization of this community. To the extent that health care institutions, educational institutions, mass media systems, industrial and commercial enterprises, law enforcement and regulatory agencies, as well as cultural, religious, social, and other voluntary organizations, for example, fall under the control not of black individuals but of the black community and a collective black agenda, power, and resources will have been redistributed. Even those systems which are exogenous to the community, but impinge on the lives of its members must become accountable to them, if their human/system interactions are to be helpful.

These recommendations constitute an empirical basis for public health initiatives based on cultural relativity, ecological systems change, and support for human diversity and independence. The measurement of relative or incremental success in the attainment of public health objectives, inspired by this discussion, cannot be anchored on individual attitude and behavior change. An evaluation methodology that would support the outcomes recommended here must be prepared to conduct baseline assessments of the degree to which communities are dominated and excluded. Shifts in our acquisition of power and resources, our evolving systemic capacity to participate in self-reliant and proportionately enfranchised ways can then be documented as successes.

2

School-Based Adolescent Drug Prevention: What Works and What Doesn't Work, What's Next?

Nancy S. Tobler, Ph.D.

As extensive research over the past 20 years has indicated, the abuse of cigarettes, alcohol, and other drugs has been and remains a major public health problem for adolescents in this country. In 1986, the National Senior Survey (Bachman, Johnston and O'Malley, 1987) indicated that more than 90 percent of high school seniors had had alcoholic beverages to drink and over 65 percent were current users (i.e., had drunk alcoholic beverages during the last 30 days). Further, two-thirds of all seniors had smoked cigarettes and 30 percent were current smokers.

In a study conducted for the National Institute on Drug Abuse (NIDA, 1989), it was found that alcohol continues to be the drug of choice among adolescents. Half of all youth aged 12 to 17 years had used alcohol, and 25 percent were current users of alcohol. Almost as many adolescents had experimented with cigarettes as with alcohol, but only half as many (12 percent) reported that they had smoked cigarettes in the month previous to the survey. Marijuana was the third most commonly used drug (17 percent had ever used it; 6 percent were current users), followed closely by smokeless tobacco.

Prevention Practices and Theory

Prevention efforts have changed substantially over time as researchers have begun to develop different models based on knowledge of human development and of children's and adolescents' drug use experiences. Drug education programs in the 1960s focused on instilling fear of the consequences of drug use. In the 1970s, prevention programs focused on providing accurate and complete information on drug use as well as on personal and social development. For example, affective education programs were designed to help youth develop skills to enhance self-esteem, problem-solving, decision-making, and interpersonal communication.

A more recent approach incorporates features from these earlier models and also emphasizes the relationships between individuals' psychosocial development and environmental influences. Resistance skills—how to say NO—are an important component of this approach, which strives to promote personal and social competence generally and with regard to situations such as the temptation to use alcohol and other drugs.

In a 1987 synthesis of research on school-based prevention programs, Klitzner concluded that a community-wide, "comprehensive approach to prevention involving the school, parents, youth and the community" held the most promise for reducing youth alcohol and other drug use. In the synthesis, he described a particular need for emphasis on well-planned implementation of comprehensive programs, with a greater emphasis on school policy, parent involvement, and specific strategies for reaching youth at high risk for drug use (Klitzner, 1987). The vast majority of researchers and practitioners today agree that comprehensive prevention programs are most likely to be successful.

In short, then, research findings suggest that the most effective prevention programs would be those that combine cognitive, affective, and skills development approaches and are comprehensive in that they reach all students and involve the entire community (including the school, youth, parents, community agencies and organizations, and other segments of the community). While most school districts across the country were providing prevention programs for students before 1986, there is evidence to indicate that these programs were limited in terms of the numbers and types of students they reached and the comprehensiveness of their prevention approaches.

Prior to the enactment of the Drug Free Schools and Communities Act (DFSCA) in 1986, as many as 90 percent of school districts across the country reported that drug prevention was taught in their local schools. However, such instruction was generally not provided at all grade levels, nor at any one specific grade level (although junior high students were the most commonly targeted age group). Further, less than three-quarters of school districts had adopted written drug abuse policies, and few districts reported taking actions in conjunction with drug offenses in the 1986-87 school year, according to a Congressionally mandated study by Chaney and Farris (1987). Most districts taught students "about the causes and effects of substance abuse, about ways to *improve* self-esteem, and about laws regarding substance abuse." Almost 90 percent of districts also offered "training in resisting peer pressure" as part of their prevention programs. However, less than half of all districts offered services aimed specifically at youth considered to be at high risk for alcohol and other drug use. Chaney and Farris also reported that local districts devoted only limited resources to drug prevention. "Ninety-one percent reported no central office staff working full-time on substance abuse education; and 28 percent had neither full-time nor part-time staff" with responsibility for drug use prevention.

The Drug Free Schools and Communities Act

In response to the increased awareness of alcohol and other drug abuse among youth, Congress enacted the DFSCA to expand and strengthen drug and alcohol abuse education and prevention programs in communities throughout the nation. The President and Congress designed the DFSCA State and Local Grants Program to encourage and support broadly-based cooperation among schools, communities, parents, and governmental agencies to bring the nation significantly closer to the goal of a drug-free generation and a drug-free society. Congress has reaffirmed its belief in the critical role of these various agencies in achieving this goal through subsequent legislative amendments and by progressively increasing program resources. In FY 1990, a total of $460,554,000 was available to support the efforts of these state and local programs; and for FY 1991, $497,709,000 was appropriated.

The U.S. Department of Education is responsible for administering the DFSCA and the Department annually distributes DFSCA funds to the states via the state education agencies (SEAs) and the Governors' offices. Each SEA must allot approximately 90 percent of the funds it receives to local education agencies (LEAs) to improve alcohol and other drug use education, prevention, early intervention, and rehabilitation referral programs. SEAs may use the remaining 10 percent of the funds for administrative activities and/or to supplement the grants to LEAs. The Governors' offices provide financial support for anti-drug abuse efforts to parent groups, community-based organizations, or other public or private nonprofit entities. At least 42.5 percent of the Governors' funds must be used for programs for youth at high risk for alcohol and other drug use (as defined in the Act).

In the last ten years we have learned what makes successful drug prevention programs. Unfortunately, the majority of programs offered in the schools throughout the United States are *not* the recently identified successful research-based programs. Despite evidence from a five-year statewide study (Hopkins, Mauss, Kearney and Weisheit, 1988) showing that the "Here's Looking At You, Two" program did not impact drug use, it was adopted in five states (Chaney, Farris and Westat, 1988). Also, "Project DARE" reaches 70 percent of our nation's school districts as stated by President Clinton in a proclamation for National DARE Day. Unfortunately, Project DARE has been only marginally effective in decreasing drug use (Ennett, Tobler, Ringwalt and Flewelling, 1994). However, we do have school-based drug prevention programs that change adolescent drug use behaviors. A meta-analysis of 120 programs showed that the more *participatory* programs that increase interpersonal skills were successful across cigarettes, alcohol, marijuana, and other illicit drugs, and with minority populations (Tobler and Stratton, in press). The findings from this meta-analysis do not stand alone, but are supported by many other reviews (Bangert-Drowns, 1988; Botvin, 1990; Bosworth and Sailes, 1993; Brown and Caston, in press; Hansen, 1992).

The following summary presents a brief overview of the meta-analysis that supports the efficacy of certain drug prevention programs. Using self-reported drug use measures, a meta-analysis of 120 school-based experimental/quasi-experimental adolescent drug prevention programs (5th-12th grade) were examined for commonalties in program content and program delivery (Tobler and Stratton, 1996). Meta-analysis, a scientifically rigorous method of integrating research findings, was used to compare effectiveness across programs. Quantitative synthesis was accomplished by computing an effect size which is the standardized mean difference between the intervention and comparison groups. Unlike significance tests, the effect size allows comparisons across studies having varied sample size.

Type of Program

Based on their content and delivery, two types of programs were identified: Non-Interactive (Knowledge-Only, Affective-Only, Knowledge-Plus-Affective) and Interactive programs (Social Influences, Comprehensive Like Skills, Others). Two Non-Interactive programs (Knowledge-Only and Affective-Only) and one Interactive program (Others) will not be discussed because of limited numbers. The seventy-five Interactive programs were significantly more effective than the forty-five Non-Interactive programs ($p = .05$).

Content

The content of the unsuccessful non-interactive programs had an *intra*personal focus. Two theoretical assumptions were reflected. First, the "Values" programs encouraged examination of one's personal beliefs, values, and decision-making patterns. These programs encouraged the adolescents to make a personal decision to abstain from using drugs based on ethical or moral considerations. The content was directed at the person and his internal perceptions, not those of his peers. These approaches were particularly ineffective.

The second group of non-interactive programs, called the "DARE Type," focused on ways to strengthen the individual's personal competence and intrapersonal functioning to forestall involvement with drugs. Self-esteem building, decision making, and coping skills were included along with public commitment activities. Although more effective than the values programs, the DARE type were still significantly less effective than the Interactive programs.

Developmentally, the intrapersonal focus with its goal of increasing self-esteem may have greater potential in the elementary grades where students are in self-contained classrooms. Having a single teacher allows greater individual attention and recognition. Whereas, the middle or junior high school programs that focus on self-esteem can be problematic as teachers can be involved with upwards of 120 adolescents in a day.

All the successful interactive programs focused primarily on *inter*personal competence and some added additional *intra*personal skills (1996) (e.g., goal setting, coping skills). Knowledge about the long- and short-term consequences of drug use and prodrug media influences were combined with drug refusal skills and other *inter*personal skills. Perceptions of peer drug use were challenged by providing feedback from local school drug use surveys. Drug refusal skills were used to enable skillful negotiation of drug offers so that the adolescent can continue to feel secure in his/her peer group when refusing.

Delivery

The non-interactive group process is familiar to all teachers. Lectures were used to deliver the content. Some programs combined didactic presentations with discussions and experiential activities. However, communications were mostly between the teacher and student, not student to student.

On the other hand, the interactive programs used a very different way of learning. The interactive process provided contact, intercommunication, and opportunities for exchange of ideas. The interactions included everyone and were both *participatory* and *between peers*. Structured small group activities were used to introduce program content and promote the acquisition of drug refusal skills. It is hoped that by receiving corrective comments in a supportive atmosphere the youth would be able to use their new skills in a situation of higher stress (i.e., a real world, drug-related situation).

Adolescence is a period during which the establishment of peer relationships takes priority over adult relationships. Groups offer support and define reality for adolescents and, in the case of drug prevention, furnish an excellent opportunity to challenge the almost universal tendency of adolescents to overestimate the amount of drug use by their peers. It comes as no surprise that the interactive programs which are based on peer-to-peer exchanges are more effective than the non-interactive programs which depend upon an ethical decision or personal change of values.

A succinct list of what works and what doesn't work in school-based adolescent drug prevention programs is shown in Tables 1 and 2.

Caveat

A large drop in the effectiveness was observed for all programs when implemented on a large scale (over 400 youth) but the large interactive programs were still significantly superior to the large non-interactive programs ($p = .05$). A number of possible explanations exist. Ideally, everyone participates. In large scale implementations, extra leaders are

Table 1
What Works in School-Based Adolescent Drug Prevention

CONTENT

Knowledge
- Long-term physical and psychological consequences of drug use
- Short term effects such as cigarette breath or car accidents

Attitudes
- Feedback from school surveys on estimates of friends use
- Correction of perception of universal peer use
- Media and social influences that create prodrug attitudes

***Inter*personal Skills**
- Drug refusal skills
- Assertiveness skills
- Communication skills
- Safety skills (i.e., ways to intervene in drinking/driving situations, etc.)

***Intra*personal Skills if Combined with Interpersonal Skills**
- Self-esteem building
- Coping skills
- Stress reduction techniques
- Goal setting
- Decision/problem solving

DELIVERY

- *Participatory*
- *Everyone* included
- Structured activities to promote interaction *between* peers
- *Rehearsal* of drug refusal skills
- Role plays that are *student generated*
- Sufficient *practice* time
- Peer *modeling* of appropriate behavior
- *Supportive* comments from group

Table 2
What Doesn't Work in School-Based Adolescent Drug Prevention

CONTENT

Knowledge
- Programs lacking a knowledge component
- Media and social influences not addressed

Attitudes
- Values
- Ethical/moral decision-making

***Inter*personal skills**
- Drug refusal skills omitted

***Intra*personal skills without *Inter*personal skills**
- Solely self-esteem building
- Self-esteem combined with ethical/moral decisions
- Solely intrapersonal focus
- Goal setting
- Coping skills
- Stress reduction

DELIVERY

- Unstructured talk sessions
- Lectures
- Teacher centered class discussions
- Passive participation

---

seldom provided to subdivide classes into smaller groups. Naturally, programs providing small groups have a greater opportunity for *each* adolescent to practice, become comfortable with, and gain proficiency in using new skills. Without extra leaders to facilitate small groups, a particular adolescent can potentially interact only a few times. The adolescent doesn't get his "AIR TIME" and an essential part of the program is missing. A second cause may be that some teachers did not include all parts of the program equally, possibly because they felt uncomfortable with certain areas such as role playing. Teachers need training to be convinced that this type of program works as well as to learn the necessary skills (Botvin, Filazolla and Botvin, 1990). Another possibility may be that drug prevention does not differ from other education goals that are negatively related to school size and the number of schools in the districts (Fowler and Walberg, 1991).

Attitudes and Use

Explaining the pathways that lead to behavioral change helps to strengthen the findings. The "Monitoring the Future Study" found that as the perceived risk of using marijuana increases, there were associated decreases in the use of marijuana (Bachman, Johnston and O'Malley, 1991). Preceding the recent increases in marijuana use, decreases in the perceived harm of marijuana use were observed (Johnston, O'Malley and Bachman, 1995). It follows that programs able to change youth attitudes about drug use will be more effective. The interactive programs did show significant positive changes for knowledge and attitudes as well as decreases in drug use. Conversely, the non-interactive programs were not able to show significant positive changes for attitudes or for drug use, although they did show gains for knowledge. Neither showed changes for self-esteem, but this was not theorized as a mechanism for change with the interactive programs.

Intensity

The average time spent on 68 percent of the programs was just six hours. The longer programs with an average of 18 hours did slightly better. Only 16 programs offered boosters, and just four provided more than one year of boosters. It is remarkable that such low intensity programs produced behavioral effects. This stands in contrast to the School Health Education Evaluation that found nearly 30 hours of instruction were needed to show behavioral changes (Connell, Turner and Mason, 1985).

Clinical Success

The interactive programs were equally successful with cigarettes, alcohol, marijuana, and illicit drugs *and* in minority schools. The interactive programs had an effect size of .20, while the non-interactive programs had an effect size of .02. Were these modest effects of real importance?

The study of the effects of aspirin on heart attacks, a randomized double-blind study which involved 22,000 doctors, was canceled because it was considered unethical to not offer the treatment to the control group (Rosenthal, 1994). The success rate of that study was 3.5 percent. The interactive programs had a success rate of 9.5 percent, while the non-interactive programs found in the majority of our schools had a success rate of 1.0 percent. The difference of 8.5 percent between the interactive and non-interactive programs is clearly a clinically significant finding, particularly when the mean delivery intensity of all programs was just 10 hours. It would be startling if this figure could be changed to the exact number of lives that would be affected, but that would depend on too many assumptions. What is relevant is that the medical community now recommends that all senior citizens take an aspirin a day. Then why aren't we providing interactive programs that are 8.5 percent more successful than what our youth are receiving now? The policy question is not whether prevention programs work. Rather, can the successful programs increase their effectiveness? This may be possible if policy makers/school administrators/teachers are willing to:

- Guide and support the implementation of interactive groups. This requires a paradigm shift from "instructing classes" to "facilitating groups."
- Realize that the majority of the successful programs are developmentally appropriate for junior high youth and will not maintain their appeal or effectiveness with high school youth. Funding is needed to develop and test innovative high school programs that realistically deal with adolescent use and, in many cases, abuse of drugs.
- Undertake aggressive teacher training needed in order to implement a truly interactive group. This should be initiated in both the teachers' colleges and with present teachers.
- Provide funding in a manner that will insure that long term goals are met. For example, discontinue the practice of short-term funding with mandates that force administrators to address certain grades, subjects or populations.

- Drop the unrealistic expectations of long term results from low intensity (10 hr) programs given once in junior high. Instead, fund programs that have grade appropriate yearly boosters to increase program intensity to a "critical mass."

3

Substance Abuse, Violence, and Crime

Alberto G. Mata, Jr., Ph.D.

There is rarely a day where substance abuse is not linked to personal tragedy, impacting someone in their home (Saltzman, Mercey and Rosenberg, 1990), marking school, workplace, or otherwise further testing our social fabric and community quality of life (Mercey and Houck, 1988; NIJ Journal, 1995). Further complicating this situation, in toll and in wake, are gangs and violence. While other types of crimes are declining, those involving interpersonal violence—assault, rape and homicide, for example—are rising (Blumstein, 1994). It is not very difficult to convince most Americans that violence is a serious problem confronting most of our communities (Riess and Roth, 1993; Harris, 1988). While awaiting national and state leadership's steps towards a measured response, it is a problem that cannot be ignored at the community level (CDC, 1986; Griffin and Bell, 1989; Snyder, Sickmund and Poe-Yamagata, 1996).

While the persisting problem of substance abuse—tobacco, alcohol, and illicit drugs—remains a key concern and issue for many in our respective communities, there is growing understanding of how substance abuse interacts and compounds with the problem of violence (Burns, 1980; Johnson, et al., 1990), and also how it is connected with many facets of interpersonal aggression and violence (Curtis, 1975; Chaiken and Chaiken, 1990). This essay addresses the question of gangs, drugs, and violence. Youth's increasing involvement with drugs and violence needs to be placed with a broader discussion of violence. The paper suggests that violence (i.e., assault, rape, robbery, and homicide) is no longer just a primary responsibility with which the criminal justice system must wrestle. Like HIV, child abuse, and domestic violence, any efforts to stem youth gang-related violence will require collaborative and cooperative efforts between (1) helping and social service professionals, (2) the researcher community, (3) community based organizations (CBOs), and (4) policy planning and programming officials. This paper will close with a discussion of suggested issues that such meaningful collaborative and cooperative effort must consider and address.

While it is important to treat, care, and provide services to those individuals and families impacted by substance abuse, there is also much to be gained by lessening further spread, lessening increasing consequences, and reducing the likelihood of this problem becoming the inheritance passed on to the next generation (Sampson, 1987). And so, it does not take a great leap of faith to see that prevention, early intervention, and health promotion are also wise investments of time, limited staff, and resources (Cohen, 1994). Yet, economic uncertainty, fiscal crises, and marked differences in beliefs about the proper role of government at all levels are lessening policy-makers' and leaders' involvement and support of sustained, substantive, and comprehensive early intervention and prevention programming efforts. While some will take exception to prevention programming promise, many others will herald substantive, comprehensive, and integrated prevention approach as the only measured response that may prove appropriate and meaningful (Spergel, 1995; APA, 1993; Wish and Johnson, 1986). Yet, violence prevention as collaborative and cooperative strategies is only being considered in a few of our nation's more troubled communities (Wilson and Howell, 1993; Tolan and Guerra, 1994).

While the debate in Washington continues about the proper role and extent of federal government, what priorities and whose responsibility these issues pertain, we are also witnessing the beginnings of reversals of almost a decade of evolving prevention policy and practice. This comes at a time when one is encountering a reluctance to further burden a shrinking local economy base and increase need for additional tax revenues. But the problems, issues, and challenges have not abated. The new congress has already taken major steps to rescind support, resources, and leadership for targeted gang, drug, and violence prevention initiatives; communities looking for federal support can come to expect less than what they enjoyed in the recent past decade. Nonetheless, many of our communities, neighborhoods, and families will be left alone to contend and wrestle with the problems of drugs, violence, and

HIV/AIDS wrought on their respective families, schools, communities, and work sites.

It is not bold or new to demonstrate the many links of substance abuse to problems of poverty (McGeary, 1988), crime (Wolfgang and Wiener, 1982; Tonry and Wilson, 1990), racism (Siberman, 1978), sexism (National Research Council, 1993) and growing alienation (Jencks and Meyers, 1990). Nor is it challenging to posit that many in this "New Congress" believe that they have little responsibility or concern for those affected by these problems. A cursory summary of basic tenets would suggest that they believe in a "limited government role, a balanced budget, the return of greater control and influence to state and local government, revitalization of traditional family values and promoting a greater sense of self-reliance and personal responsibility" as better solutions than what they have seen over the past decades of a Democratic Party-controlled congress.

Yet, there is little to suggest what they recommend for maintaining or insuring the further decline in our country's standard of living and quality of life, for handling measures to deal with economic challenges. While many would scrap our current provisions for "social welfare," reinstitute church as the key source for social welfare provisions, replace child welfare with orphanages, and call for greater self-help efforts and voluntarism, there is little in their agenda about what to do with gangs and drugs or the victims of violence. Of no less concern is the fact that one finds little in their agenda as to what they would recommend for assisting our respective communities to meet the challenge of violence and substance abuse.

Also while the new congress's "Contract with America" calls for local control, it is not clear where local community based initiatives, programs, and organizations fit in "the new contract adherent's vision, mission and directives." Their sense of the safety net does not extend to the wide needs that many CBOs provide to substance abusers, their respective families and communities, their victims, victims' families, and significant others. Other than the embracing of an occasional poster person of the year, many Contract with America adherents do not have a true appreciation about resilience in spite of their success in coping with adversity. It is not that they are wholly unfamiliar with resiliency and its importance for policy and programming, for they do celebrate these individuals. One will have to look hard to find in their policy and programming efforts about what they posit for promoting and stimulating youth's resiliency and hardiness. In fact, other than cursory mention in late 1980s legislation, both sides of the Hill have yet to fully support and encourage measures and policies that promote personal, familial, and community resiliency.

In short, their Contract seems to have little sense of the problems and urgencies that many of the CBOs, their staff, and respective agencies contend with *on a daily basis and year after year*! At state and county levels other than what can be cut from current programming efforts, new Contract adherents do not provide any sense of who will be responsible for paying for new metal detectors in courts and schools, or for expanded jails and prison budgets. One finds in their ranks few proponents for adding violence prevention initiatives to their agendas. Yet the tasks, challenges, and issues remain (Jagger and Deitz, 1987). They remain formidable, growing, serious, and energy-absorbing ones.

Yet, as HIV/AIDS and violence epidemic enjoins what some term "an American disease" (Musto, 1973), our society's use and misuse of illicit substances, including alcohol and tobacco products, many are now wondering when something will be done about the turmoil that turns many fellow citizens' homes inside out (Wintemute, Teret, Kraus and Wright, 1992; Zimring, 1989). The conflict and turbulence that marks school life for many pupils, teachers, and administrators have been well documented (Jencks and Meyers, 1990; Garafalo, Siegel and Laub, 1987). The apparently senseless carnage that marks many inner city neighborhoods (Hamid, 1990; Griffin and Bell, 1989) and involves many of our nation's low SES minority youth (Curtis, 1975; Fingerhut, et al., 1991) poses a national threat. The numbers of apparently "random acts of violence once thought only to mark those mean streets" (Fingerhut, et al., 1991), has caused serious concern in many workplaces and extends to rural settings (Zimring 1991)!

For many of our colleagues directing and working in CBOs, preventive violence efforts are novel and may involve a stretch. For many of these colleagues, violence prevention becomes one more thing that needs to be done, but again with less than adequate resources, time, personnel, and support! While some of my colleagues have said, "Oh, no, what else do they want us to add to our agenda, yet provide one with little direction or resources to carry it out." Others have commented that adding violence to their agenda without additional staff and resources will only serve to overextend them. It is not that they are unconcerned with violence prevention programming efforts, but that they are concerned with the need to balance it vis-à-vis other commitments, obligations, and responsibilities.

But the problem of violence and substance abuse is a concern that we can no longer ignore. It cannot be left up to tomorrow's priorities or for someone else to take on. It is a concern of the children, their families, and neighbors in our respective communities. It is a concern that extends from our troubled youth's homes and spills unto our schools, work places, and centers of community life. The growth of this problem is such that front-line criminal justice system (CJS), Health and Human Services (HHS), and other professionals called to curb, control and ameliorate its more provoking, deleterious acts and consequences, *see it no longer as just their province*. They too call for community support and collaboration.

It needs to build on past and current community collaborative efforts and reflect a network of social support and services! Thus, it requires us to take stock of past and current efforts and endeavors. It needs to lead to the development of a measured response that is "within our reach of existing leadership, organizations, resources and resolve" (Schorr, 1988). It is an issue that, on any given day, will require a whole range of professionals, paraprofessionals, volunteers, indigenous leaders, and wiser use of existing time, staff, and resources.

I will now turn to issues, dimensions, and questions that shape current debate and thinking as it concerns making violence a public health and community concern.

On Violence and Substance Abuse

In a benchmark essay, Dr. Mark Rosenberg and James Mercey challenge their peers—health and public health professionals—to see and embrace violence as a public health concern. Those working with underserved populations and high-risk countries need to seriously consider their position, understandings, and suggestions for points of collaboration. While they too acknowledge that violence is of a growing nature and consequence, they decry the view that it is unpredictable, unpreventable, and "another fact of life" American citizens and society must endure (Rosenberg, 1990; Ruttenberg, 1994; Mercey and Houck, 1988).

Rosenberg and Mercey go on to say ". . . the past thirty years have witnessed a dramatic increase in homicide rates in the U.S.: in 1980 the homicide rate reached its highest recorded level in the country." In the late 1980s and early 1990s, Washington D.C., our national capital, bore the dubious distinction of being our nation's murder capital. Today, the "dismal honor" has been passed on to New Orleans. Across America's heartland one sees major increases in homicides and other index crime, especially those involving youth and young adults. In Oklahoma City on April 19, 1995, the count grew by 169 homicides. One should keep in mind that for many of our fellow citizens the less serious types of assaults and related crimes are more likely to befall them (FBI, 1995), yet it is the apparently senseless, wanton, heinous, and tragic acts that color most American attitudes about violence and what comes into their minds when they speak about it (Zimring, 1991; Allen-Hagen, Sickmund and Snyder, 1994; A. Goldstein, 1993; Horowitz, 1983; Block, 1985; Blumstein, Cohen, Roth and Visher, 1986).

Since 1986, the number of homicides and suicides has grown to numbers as large or larger than the number of American servicemen lost in Vietnam. No less troubling is the number of non-fatal assaults and suicides, which are estimated to outnumber homicides and suicides by more than a 100 to 1 ratio. In the United States, 6 in 10 homicide victims involved firearms. Of those victims, 9 in 10 were killed with a weapon, i.e., clubs, knives or firearms. Of all suicides and homicides occurring in the U.S., 6 in 10 were firearm weapons related. Except for public health officials who argue that many of these fatalities and injuries are preventable, there are few policymakers or leaders who push for serious gun control measures.

Beginning in the home and extending to our schools, workplaces, and even to centers of commerce and recreation, Rosenberg and Mercey call for the pushing of an agenda that seeks to control, reduce, and prevent the problem of interpersonal violence. In Rosenberg and Fenley's benchmark monograph (1991) they estimate that about 1 in 5 adult women have been abused by their spouse at least once.

In 1986 there were over 2 million reported cases of child abuse and neglect. These two million reported cases were a 6 percent increase over the previous year, and each year thereafter continues to increase these cases. Current research suggests few signs of any abating!

In addition to increases in domestic violence, we have seen major increases in rape every year since 1986. Rape, which the FBI considers second only to murder, increased 21 percent from 1977 to 1984. Today, it remains at levels that few communities can ignore (in many communities it is second to none). In addition to homicide, domestic violence, and rape, they also draw attention to interpersonal assault. Interpersonal assaults range from non-lethal physical assaults, sexual assaults, robbery, to serious and lethal assaults. The former remains more common, and also continues to increase. There is no doubt that these types of crimes are on the rise. In some communities, interpersonal assaults have become so serious that they become entrenched in daily concerns. In other communities, interpersonal affairs are an emergent, occasional, yet no less troubling trend in settings, context, and peoples.

In urban and rural communities, "serious beating or death of child at the hand of parent," "domestic violence," "carjacking," "home invasions," "drive-by shootings," and "gang attacks" have led many state legislatures to explore measured responses and actions. So extensive and persuasive are these acts that many states have passed less than fully considered legislation. Those legislative acts range from "three strikes and you're out" to the building of more prison facilities and other retributive measures that do little to stem current trends. Yet they promote few measures that increase support for additional staff, community correction programs, or services to deal with offender and victims. In some states, it has led to questionable knee-jerk legislation, i.e., passage of concealed weapons laws while private citizens are licensed, but the measure provides significantly less training and education than do line uniformed officers.

While homicide is the 12th leading cause of death for all Americans, homicide is the third leading cause of death for young people. For over a decade there have been reports that homicide takes its greatest toll among racial/ethnic minorities, men, and our young. A most striking characteristic is that the homicide rate for young whites and blacks is disproportionate. The young black male rate (1 in 28) is 5 times higher than young white (1 in 164) males. The rate for young black women fares no better, as it is higher than young white males. Among Afro-American males the homicide rate was almost 5 times that of their white male counterparts.

For Latinos residing in the five southwestern states of the United States, the Hispanic homicide rate (20.5 per 100,000) was two-and-a-half times the Anglo-America rate (7.9 per 100,000). There is no doubt that Latino homicides and related injuries have increased, yet the increase and causes remain open for further data and study. While many from within and without the barrio would argue that serious lethal gang-related shootings in most barrios seem to have been further aggravated by increases in drug trafficking and use, current studies remain less than unequivocal.

Rosenberg, Mercey, and their colleagues' efforts have also measured the cost of violence in terms of "general mortality and morbidity vital statistics," by controlling for age, ethnicity, urban/rural residency, SES, by indicators that measure potential years of life lost. These measures, while developing, are more likely to attract the attention of corporate and public policy officials for whom the costs of crime and homicide is not lost. Relying on all their estimates, the economic costs associated with violence ranges from $60 billion in 1988 to $200 billion in 1994. These figures need to be better developed and refined for local community use. Many times they don't catch one's eye until one speaks of personal costs, the costs to the family, and to the larger community. Before this case argument can be stated and honed, it will require better data, surveillance systems, and community awareness and education.

Although they address a wide range of issues related to violence, it is clear to Mercey and Rosenberg that alcohol and drug use are associated with this violence! While this is an enterprise that is still developing, it is clear that alcohol and drug use are associated with this violence. They have challenged researchers and policy-makers to further examine and develop our understanding of the relationship between violence and substance abuse. They specifically call for the research agenda that will provide clearer data and understanding (1) about the perpetrator and victim's use and misuse of alcohol and drugs; (2) about the form and involvement with self-destructive behaviors; (3) about the impacts and disruption on family members of perpetrators, victims, and their respective social networks and communities; (4) about data and model that county, city, and community-based agencies could use to plan, monitor and evaluate their efforts; and (5) the impact on public, national government organizations and private health, helping and social institutions.

Here they see a need to take stock of community-based leadership, programs, and services. They would like to explore with CBOs lessons learned from their substance abuse early intervention and prevention efforts and see how they might lend themselves to the development of interpersonal aggression and violence preventative measures in our homes, schools, communal institutions, and work. They don't seek to develop wholly new organization "programs," but call for efforts that begin with existing and established community based leadership, institutions, and organizing efforts.

They also draw attention to the criminal justice system and policy initiatives that could make these efforts more successful and substantive. Here they seek to acknowledge CJS's contribution and limitation; but more importantly, they call for public health, community-based organizations, and other related programs to increase their roles and contributions with CJS. At the same time they seek to encourage CJS to acknowledge the role and contribution that these "new players" potentially can provide and effect.

Drs. Rosenberg and Mercey note that traditional federal and state public policy response for dealing with violence has been to assign primary, if not sole responsibility to the criminal justice system. As it concerns prevention, CJS's approach has generally relied on incapacitation and deterrence. Yet in the past decade and half one has witnessed an increased call for new programming efforts to complement and enhance community-oriented and community policing practices. Currently, many heads and agents of public safety and justice recognize the profound effect of current policy on their institutions, staff, and budgets. They too are aware of the need for others to work and share in this burden. They call attention to the fact that this problem is more than just a problem for the police, courts and penal system. In short, they call for the support of the criminal justice system, for sharing in the responsibility by CBOs and minority community leadership, and dialogues that serve to build new mechanisms and programs to work collaboratively.

For most of us, violence potentialities invite one and all to step back and ask what do we do when violence marks, shatters, and befalls one of ours: a neighbor, a local school, a playground, a local store, or business. Or, worse yet, impacts one from outside who was just passing by, calling on, visiting, or dropping in on. Who will respond? What will need to be done? How should they proceed? And how do we prevent the victims from being re-victimized by measures? How do we reform measures and responses that are not wholly appropriate, sensitive, fragmented and compartmentalized, and effective?

For a few, attention will be on how we may mitigate, reduce, and otherwise lessen these risks for children and families for whom these issues, situations, and consequences are part of, or at least are anticipated in, everyday life? What may one do to abate the youth's growing involvement with substance abuse and serious violence, and how might we mitigate the consequences on youth, their victims, their families and peers, and the larger society?

Clearly, there is a major need for professional health, social, and educational helping institutions' involvement and the bringing to bear of their interdisciplinary knowledge and expertise. Nonetheless, this will involve some refocusing and reframing of their roles and functions. But more important, it will inevitably warrant collaborative and cooperative efforts with CBOs and the communities that they serve.

CBOs and the Public Health Model Approach to Violence

The problem is so complex that it requires more than one approach, a major institution or a community's leadership. Even when one does not directly target violence, the meeting of unmet need with concrete help provides help to clients in a respectful and evenhanded manner and the working with and accounting to program supporters will serve to challenge the notion that no one cares and that nothing works.

Violence prevention will require that we cross traditional, professional, and bureaucratic boundaries. Our planning and programming must assure viable responsive organizational structures, yet retain some flexibility. Only when these efforts are grounded in understanding of the context of clients' lives and share in their hopes and aspirations can these programs really have a chance to improve and enhance the quality of life, safety, and opportunity to prosper.

Ending youth related homicide—the unintended firearm shootings, drivebys, revenge shootings, crime related shootings, and drug-dealing related homicides—will still need the police and CJS's primary involvement. But their policing efforts must enjoy the community leadership's input and support. Although largely the purview of police and courts, efforts to curb and reduce youth violence will require widespread community education and support of their efforts. This can, first, be achieved through community education campaigns and town hall meetings. These measures eventually will entail stimulating community's adoption of programs like community watch, silent witness, related victim assistance, restitution, and possibly mediation services.

The search for more comprehensive preventive and targeted early intervention measures is no longer limited to our urban inner city war zones. Preventing interpersonal aggressive acts escalating to homicide among our youth and young adults will, in some communities with chronic unceasing gang violence problems, require emphasis to be placed first on ending ghetto/barrio gang warfare. In other communities, emphasis will need to be placed on reducing the further spread or re-emergence of gangs and gang activities. In both, it is not simply a matter of using suppression strategies and techniques, but use of other complementary approaches and strategies as well.

Some effort must be taken to lessen their marginalization of these youth and their families. These family and their youth must be subject to socially integrative developmental efforts. It will eventually require that victim services and gang intervention programming be enhanced and expanded. And of course, efforts to secure education and employment skills and opportunities must also be developed and provided. These must include services and opportunities that they can utilize in their transition from their life with violence to life after violence.

While acknowledging the many controversies associated with male responsibility and mentoring, programs or groups like "The Muslims and the Promise Keepers" developing forums and vehicles for positive, nurturing, responsible male involvement and support models with these youth is essential. Annual gender-specific community conferences and workshops will serve to more adequately target youth concerns that are left unattended or inadequately addressed by more general approaches. There is no avoiding the question that hyper-masculine roles and sexist roles need to be challenged and meaningful alternatives developed and explored.

As in many communities, families are becoming more strained, stretched, and challenged. In such families, the emphasis may be on a campaign to lessen family and domestic violence. Concomitant with these efforts are education and early intervention services that are truly preventive in orientation and design. Family support programs would do well to add to their educational campaign. These campaigns should serve to lessen family and domestic violence that some see as only happening to others but others see as part of family life.

In the past two-and-a-half decades, the emergence of a wide range of programs dealing with various aspects of family violence have emerged, yet few programs have been developed to work with youthful violent offenders or with families with a history of gang membership. A concerted community education and intervention campaign involving key local organizations and resources has been superseded by CBO's struggle to service unmet needs and work on assuring that a continuum of services meets those needs. For sure, the targeting of those families or areas with greatest need and least resources through early education and intervention is a must. Eventually, violence prevention efforts will require the larger community's recognition that family services, support and intervention program efforts need to be enhanced and expanded! But they should not lose sight that intervention and prevention are no less needed.

Finally, there will be some need to pay attention to respond to, curb, and prevent violence from claiming more victims and their significant others. This will require that we seek to increase involvement of police and emergency hospital personnel and improve their training. The enhancement of both personnel training should serve to improve services and lessen victims' feelings of being disparaged, depreciated, or belittled.

Eventually this will lead to the implementation of programs like the Austin (Texas) Police Department's Victim Assistance and Services volunteer program. The success of these programming efforts will rest on the availability and quality of family mediation programs, victim assistance, and restitution programs to meet the present need.

In some instances there are calls for efforts to increase the children, their parents, and local leadership's resilience, hardiness, and steadfastness. Also one should note that there is a growing number of CBOs drawing attention to those hardy, resilient, and positive individuals, families, and institutions. The search for protective factors buffering individuals from exposure to risk is also poorly addressed by most helping research professions and research institutions. Research and practice professionals seek to identify factors that promote "wellness" and lessen one's risk status. While not a panacea, it should serve to promote indigenous values and lifestyles that could be supported and extended to others.

On School Settings

In schools where students' daily routines are marked by peers' serious threats of assault and related acts of violence, youth development approaches could emphasize student peer educators, conflict resolution education, after-school programs, and mediation programs. Many schools have added violence prevention and mediation to their curriculum. In more progressive school districts, the eventuality of violence has lead them to re-think the need for school health clinics and counseling programs. In some schools, student assistance programs once limited to substance abuse education are now attending to violence and aggression.

Substance Abuse, Violence, and Crime 45

Alternative schools must make all efforts to become more of a "lifelines program" than "just the next step" before final expulsion and being turned loose to the streets. Yet this problem is not just for schools to address—it should involve the immediate and larger business community.

Meaningful school reform and action will require that areas and schools that were once written off as "no man's land to lost cause schools" be reclaimed through meaningful partnerships: school to work programs, "New Future" campaigns, and higher education cooperative agreements with inner city schools. Their efforts, while indirectly addressing violence (if youth violence is meaningfully addressed), will serve to give these children hope, dreams, and a vision of a possible future. These efforts can also serve to reinvigorate the local and national sense of community and peoplehood.

Local Business Strips, Malls and Community Centers

Although it is somewhat easier to suggest what can be done about violence in the home and school, there appear to be fewer model efforts targeting neighborhood and commercial areas. Most of these efforts have been piecemeal ones: Expanding loitering law enforcement, combatting graffiti, increasing police surveillance, and pushing for curfew laws. Not surprisingly, they have not been as effective as expected in many instances. Critics note that these piecemeal efforts have only served to push the problem elsewhere, only to return once these operations cease. In malls and smaller communal areas of commerce known for crime and violence, emphasis should be on measures not unlike women's calls for taking back the night marches, San Diego senior citizens and Chicago and Los Angeles' Muslim's community watches and patrols, and more recently, Congressional and Executive branch calls for the establishing of drug-, gun-, or violence-free zones. Meaningful efforts for making schools drug-free and firearm-free zones, while not a panacea, would allow for the beginning of reclaiming schools, playgrounds, and neighborhoods. Yet, any attempt to meet this challenge will require not only crime control and prevention, but it will also require some economic revitalization and training for these area residents.

Summary

Whether one is dealing with children, adolescents, their parents, or is primarily concerned with school dropout/pushout, teen pregnancy, delinquency, adolescent health, or special needs youth, interpersonal violence and substance abuse impacts many of your clients directly and indirectly (Riess and Roth, 1993).

Youth gang violence is a problem that requires a sustained action. A measured response suited to local needs and capabilities will have to be developed. It will require careful use and adaption of lessons that CBOs have learned about community needs, capabilities, outreach, service, accountability, crossing over, and strengthening its resolve to be able to act for their own and others' betterment. The lessons gained and learned need not be sanctioned by state or national polls or surveys, nor approved by those looking to associate and lend approval of their organization or themselves.

While violence and substance abuse make the problem more complex, it will not require a wholly new organization to address this challenge (Centers for Disease Control). Nonetheless, there is a major need for community-based and nongovernmental organization involvement and leadership to deal with interpersonal violence and aggression. Collaborative and cooperative efforts relying on existing community organizations, groups, and leaders should serve to lessen learning curves, turf conflicts, and maximize use of scarce resources and staff.

Whether it be initiated at the federal, state, county, or municipal level, the contexts for action remain our homes, schools, neighborhoods, and even our place of work. Whatever the level is focused upon, our respective community leadership and organization will need to have a stake in the making of coordinated, systematic, planned, and comprehensive measures.

4

Health Promotion: Strategies for a Generation at Risk

Richard P. Keeling, M.D., and Eric L. Engstrom
Health Advocates

A Generation At Risk

The greatest health challenges facing young people in the United States are all issues of the future consequences of current health-related behaviors—choices that young men and women make, actively or passively, as they grow, learn, and develop in a complex, confusing, and changing society. As parents, clinicians, educators, and public health officers have become aware of the spectrum of options and dangers youth in America face, our ideas of childhood, adolescence, and young adulthood as phases of happy innocence, optimistic spontaneity, and limitless potential have given way to darker concepts of growing up as a risky process. We speak now, in fact, of today's young people as a generation at risk; both popular literature and legitimate social and behavioral research identify serious problems among America's children and adolescents. Parents' fears about the chances their teenagers take have extended past their perennial concerns about experimenting with alcohol, unsafe driving, and unwanted pregnancy to include sexual assault, drug addiction, and serious, life-threatening sexually transmitted disease. This year's graduation speeches in high school classes all across America are full of the same kind of worry among new graduates: the world they confront as they leave the structured environment of secondary education is, as they see it, uncertain and threatening, full of a host of ills. Foremost among the unsolved problems challenging young people, parents, and

©1991 Health Advocates

teachers alike are the difficult issues that unite medical concerns with the social, economic, and political forces in our culture, such as the epidemics of HIV/AIDS and other sexually transmitted diseases, substance abuse, sexual assault, and unwanted pregnancy—all of them related to behavior, relationships, and risk.

Confronting these challenges to future health, success, and fulfillment for young Americans demands that we come to understand the reasons behind the choices they make. How do they learn about risks, and options, and consequences? What have they come to know? What factors influence their behaviors? What messages do they hear that promote unhealthy risk-taking? What is the central structure that governs their decision-making? Our answers to these important questions must not be simple-minded, nor self-serving; it will not be enough to sigh, wring our hands, and express our personal frustration that young people do not do what we tell them. We need to find out *why*, and *how* they don't.

Knowledge and Behavior

Most research studies performed among children, adolescents, and college students in the past decade have strongly suggested that a deficiency of factual knowledge about health issues is not the primary problem. Young people, in fact, know a great deal about things like pregnancy, alcohol, drugs, and sexually transmitted disease. In the short space of a fast decade, knowledge levels about HIV/AIDS, for example, have become impressively strong among high school and college students. Unfortunately, however, it is equally clear that knowledge—whether about HIV, other sexually transmitted diseases, alcohol, drugs, sexual assault, or other behavioral issues in health—has not predictably and durably influenced behavior choices. A sequence of epidemics of sexually transmitted disease—including herpes, Human Papillomavirus Disease, and HIV/AIDS—has not resulted in significant, predictable changes in sexual behavior among teenagers and young adults. The simple truth is that young people do not *do* what they *know*. A slightly more complex truth, of course, is that many people far older than high school age do not reliably do what they know, either—and the role modeling that occurs in that behavioral gap among older adults may have real influence on the choices made by younger men and women.

We must understand this disparity between knowledge and behavior. Traditional explanations—a sense of invincibility associated with psychological development ("it can't happen to me"), or the presence of peer pressure, for example—are probably insufficient. Social and behavioral research suggests the strong influence of a number of other factors, including feelings (perhaps one does what one feels, rather than what one knows); the absence of practical skills (young people who know what to do may not know how to do it, in a "real world" sense); previous life experiences with psychological consequences (such as sexual abuse, or living with alcoholic or dysfunctional parents) that impair concepts of self and healthy intimacy; and the absence of an effective, powerful sense of identity. Levels of self-esteem and self-determination among our teenagers are dangerously low; by the time of graduation from high school, only a minority of men and a distressingly small minority of women still feel comfortable with themselves and confident in their own abilities. Perhaps they do not do what they know because they have lost track of who they are—and, lacking a clear, internalized sense of value and a firm grasp on what they want for themselves, they have little strength to make difficult choices.

The Cultural Context of Choice

The choices that must be made, of course, occur in a fast-paced, exciting, stimulating environment with a multiplicity of sources of information. Our young people live in an educationally advanced society with tremendous technical advantages and extraordinary resources. They have learned much in a culture that handles information with incredible efficiency; satellites and cables bring the world to the classroom and the home with a remarkable sense of immediacy and currency. We all feel amazed at the increasing capability of faster microprocessors, more elaborate telecommunications equipment, and more inclusive databases. At the same time, sliding trends in averaged standardized testing scores, unevenness in basic literacy skills, and persistently troubling high school dropout rates raise real concerns about the effectiveness and relevance of our traditional educational systems. Educational theorists postulate that styles of learning have shifted in a dramatic way over the past two decades; the children and adolescents of the 1980s and 1990s learn more visually—and less from printed materials—than their predecessors. Images dominate learning. Television, video games, interactive computer software, videocassette recordings, and bright, colorful graphics have become the key tools. It seems that young people grow up learning by seeing and watching, more than by reading. Perhaps they learn to do what they see, rather than what they read, and clearly what they see is different from what they know.

We may say what we think, believe, and hope for from the pulpit, the podium, the front of the classroom, or the chair at the dining room table, but we will *do* what we truly value. Young men and women, growing up and watching their peers, their parents, leaders in their communities, and the culture around them, observe in action a value system which often differs from the one they hear about. "Just say no," we tell them; "say no to sex, to alcohol, to drugs." But at the same time the images of society's communications systems give them a very different set of messages. Advertising, prime time television, music television, music videos, motion pictures, and rock and rap music commonly equate happiness and success on the one hand with sexuality, sensuality, attractiveness, and image consciousness on the other. Over and over again, 1600 to 1800 times a week, they see society teach its values by how it sells; they listen to (or, more correctly, watch) the voices of our culture drawing for them parameters of behavior and acceptance in its entertainment, the lives of its sports figures and rock and rap stars, and the careers of its political leaders. The AAA Traffic Safety Foundation estimates that by age 18, American youth have seen more than 100,000 television commercials for beer products. In all of these shows, examples, and images, young men and women find standards against which they compare themselves in their search to fit in, to be approved and accepted. The repetition is numbing; the net effect is to build a framework that defines appropriate and acceptable behavior.

The combination of forces we have identified is potent and destructive. In the presence of eroding and unstable self-esteem, young people confront a continuous barrage of cultural messages that challenge and undermine the kinds of behavioral instruction they receive in health education, religious training, or parental conferences. Having adapted to a visually-based system of learning where images have great power, they encounter a never-ending, relentless procession of enticing, seductive images in entertainment and advertising that connect risk-taking, experimentation, sexual gratification, and substance use to happiness, attractiveness, pleasure, and success. With an unstable and floating sense of self and identity, they easily adopt the pre-packaged patterns of behavior seen among their peers, or among the imaginary peers broadcast into their consciousness. Those youth who attempt to steer their own course through this cultural maze are frequently paralyzed by a lack of skills with which to translate their knowledge into action; they discover passivity, criticism, or resistance from other members of their young community when they seek support for healthier, more self-determined choices. In the rapid pace of a sound-bite world, the gradual acquisition of wisdom through consultation and experience seems an anachronism; things need to happen more quickly than books, teachers, and schools can apparently support.

Having come to this much more complex and unsettling understanding of the diverse and powerful forces at play in shaping behavior choices among young people, we recognize that problems like HIV/AIDS or unwanted pregnancy are, in fact, not just medical or public health issues, but truly problems in a troubled culture. We see that behavior is determined by factors far beyond facts and information, far beyond an individual home or school, and far beyond the simplistic messages of instruction to "just say no." Our children have, in an important and meaningful way, become victims of the society that has tried to provide them so much, so fast, so attractively. In a social and behavioral sense, we have met the enemy, and he is us.

Perspectives on Solutions: Thinking Globally, Acting Locally

Finding solutions and promoting safety for these generations at risk will, then, be a much more complicated business than telling them more facts. Education must be much broader than disseminating information. Although the massive scope of the cultural issues may seem daunting and overwhelming, we must address them—thinking, perhaps, globally while acting locally. The three critical needs for health promotion in schools, families, clinics, treatment centers, colleges, and workplaces over the coming ten years will be to build skills, nurture and heal self-esteem, and generate support from a community of connected individuals who care about each other as they do about themselves.

Build Skills

Today's young people need practical strategies for negotiating their way through the choices they have and the dangers they face. It isn't enough to tell them to say "no"; we need to tell them how. Skill-building programs, likely dependent on participation and teaching by peers, will, through practice and reinforcement, allow young men and women to figure out ways to handle situations, negotiate agreements about behavior, respond to challenges, and get themselves out of threatening or uncertain circumstances. Over and over again, they need to practice: "What do you say to him when he wants to have sex and you don't?" Youth need to know less about the specifics of sexually transmitted diseases and their symptoms than about what to do in a tough spot on Friday night. They have less need to identify microscopic images of viruses and bacteria than to be able to understand, interpret, and discount the seductive images that surround them in a colorful and sensual world.

Nurture and Heal Self-Esteem

Young people need internal standards of behavior, based on clear and conscious senses of self. They need to know who they are, what they want for themselves, and how to find paths in the right direction. Although some adolescents and young adults can enhance their self-esteem and solidify self-determination through education and affirmation, for many, improving self-esteem will be a healing process that may require counseling or psychotherapy. The damaged self-esteem of a teenager who is the survivor of childhood sexual abuse will not respond simply to simpleminded "I'm OK, you're OK" tactics. As parents and teachers, it is essential that we begin to develop, implement, and evaluate comprehensive school health programs that focus on developing broadly defined life skills, based on self-esteem. These programs and activities may vary from place to place—but such variations should be responsive to the needs of the young people involved, and not to the fears, prejudices, or reservations of their parents. We need careful needs assessments, good curriculum planning, helpful parent involvement, and a deep, solid commitment of resources, heart, and soul from our schools. Every one of our children is an incredibly valuable resource; nurturing the greatest sense of self and health in each one is surely the most important shared responsibility of parent and teacher.

Generate Community Support

Building a healthy sense of community is crucial to the success of building skills and nurturing self-esteem. Young men and women need a sense of fitting in and being involved with a community of people who, through a spirit of healthy connectedness, care about each other and support healthy behaviors and decisions. Developing this kind of community will require leadership from young people, their parents, and their schools. In an age of isolation and separation, it means building structures for re-uniting young people to each other—not just to have them look alike, or act alike, or talk and dress alike, but to have them find value in each other and affirmation in their connectedness. Recognizing the developmental realities of teenagers and young adults and the limitations that the forces of psychological maturation put on their ability to find their own structures for healthy intimacy, we will need to involve parents, teachers, clergy, community leaders, and many others in generating a flexible, plentiful network of support and caring. Challenging isolation, competitiveness, prejudice, and bigotry will build community, connectedness, healthy intimacy, and a strong atmosphere of support for healthier behaviors.

Conclusion

This, then, is our agenda: to think globally about the challenges that have created so many dangers for this generation at risk, recognizing the roots of these problems in our culture itself; to act locally, and with vision and decisiveness, to build skills, nurture and heal self-esteem, and provide strong support; and to be truly involved in connecting our communities as caring networks of concerned people. This program is both more complicated and more satisfying than just talking facts; it is infinitely more controversial than telling young people to "just say no." But if life, and health, and future are our agenda for them—then skills, self-esteem, and support have to be the agenda for us.

5

Developing an Infrastructure for Community Prevention

Darlind J. Davis and Michael R.J. Felix

The problems of alcohol, tobacco, and other drug (ATOD) use represent a complex phenomena resulting from the interplay between individual and environmental influences. The strategies, resources, policies, practices, and ultimately the collaborations required to tackle ATOD issues are as multi-faceted and complex as the problem itself.

The political and economic changes occurring throughout the nation's infrastructure present a good news/bad news scenario for the implementation of more promising solutions to ATOD problems. The good news is that policy-makers at all levels are beginning to recognize and support locally-based constituency building as a strategy for solving multiple kinds of health and human service issues as well as ATOD problems. The bad news is political and economic expectations for this approach as a quick fix place unrealistic demands on the cadre of volunteers that seek to find long-term solutions to these complicated problems.

Angry, discordant, and frequently disenfranchised populations are making policy in the empowerment models that will be discussed. The negative side of community activism is that political outcomes may not always be consistent with accepted program practices or choices that would be made by a core policy group. Community empowerment strategies take more time than staff-driven approaches. The process of involving the grassroots in making decisions and supporting system change is a tall order and not without internal conflict, political grandstanding, and interference. Enlightened community coalitions must, however, recognize that the larger stage brings greater opportunity with the equal risk. The challenge is to continue the dialogue, regardless of the initial lack of support, and move the process to a higher level of inquiry and action. Communities experiencing the devastation of drug abuse and alcoholism and its subsequent violence to the family, school and community, feel they have little to gain by giving in.

Policy-makers have not come to reconcile that resources to support these efforts require the same long-term thrust as does local constituency-building. The nation's budget deficit and its far reaching implications on health and human service provision at local levels places ATOD constituency-building approaches in competition with other health and human service issues for scarce human and financial resources. Decision-making around services and priorities for the community is both economic and political.

There is another major challenge to bringing about long-term systemic change. That challenge is the lack of coordination among the public and private sectors throughout the United States. Specifically, government and philanthropy fund millions of dollars in demonstration programs on a national basis. Yet, long-term change is exacerbated by the lack of real cohesive coordination among the public and private sectors. Often, philanthropic organizations will implement funding programs aimed at changing a community's political, social, economic, and health infrastructure without regard to other public or private sector initiatives currently in place. The other problem is that these efforts may only derive short-term benefits as they may not impact on policy beyond their own geographical area or content issue.

The authors will argue that these challenges can be viewed as opportunities to prevent alcohol, tobacco, and other drug abuse through constituency-building and greater collaboration between public and private agencies. Building a local, voluntary constituency is an essential component to the alteration of environmental influences on drug-related behaviors. Community development involves the empowerment of everyday citizens and grassroots leadership in forcing changes in systems as well as individual behaviors in the community.

Empowerment is both a political and economic phenomenon which, when used in the context of a health paradigm, can change health status in a given population. Partnerships at all levels of American society are necessary to build necessary solutions to ATOD problems as well as many other types of health and human service issues. In order for these approaches to work, partnerships must come to recognize and support local-based constituency building and its potential to change the political, economic, social, and health landscape of America.

Constituency Building as Part of Alcohol and Drug Prevention: Political and Economic Benefits to the Community

The emerging trend in local constituency-based problem solving involves the knowledge and application of a community's health status towards resource allocation, practice implementation, and service integration. Tarlov and Felix (in press) describe the interaction of psychosocial and ecological determinants to the problems of alcohol, tobacco, and other drug problems. For each of the five levels of determinants, this health production model presents a health production strategy integrating health care, prevention, health promotion, environmental protection, and (critically) adjustments in the social infrastructure of society. They suggest that where community activism is at work, the process will drive the economic and political discussions, be they at the local, state, or national level. Perhaps more than any other problems facing communities today, the use of an empowerment model such as this has been effectively utilized in the prevention of ATOD problems. Political influence (generally regarded as politics with a small "p") is at the core of community empowerment. Community members must themselves alter the conditions that persist.

Conducting such an analysis of communities places attention on the economic and political issues in the context of the social and health conditions of a population. For example, grassroots input will be the keystone to developing local priorities for funding and services. Empowerment strategies such as these will produce perhaps the strongest attempt to prevent ATOD problems on such a large scale, especially for long-term results. This model requires the community members to be at the table. Their ability to master the political implications of health services delivery and the modification of the current infrastructure is at the base of this shift from a delivery of services model to a true empowerment methodology.

According to a recent study by the Center on Addiction and Substance Abuse (CASA) at Columbia University, the Center director, former Secretary of the U.S. Department of Health and Human Services Joseph Califano, states that skyrocketing health care costs are largely attributable to untreated alcohol, tobacco, and other drug problems. New health care reform proposals will further necessitate the need to mobilize traditionally disenfranchised populations to advocate for appropriate health and prevention services. The health needs of a population will be determined by local health status assessment. The health status assessment will provide local constituency-based groups with a current view on the overall health status of a population and all its sub-groups. This will provide a basis to measure improvements over time. It will also allow community groups to better utilize existing resources and integrate other health and human service providers as part of a community's resource mix. It will allow community groups to determine those policies that inhibit or enhance local solutions. The budget deficit and the pending change in America's health delivery system may drive the way various population groups are targeted at the community level for a variety of health and human service strategies. ATOD prevention and its subsequent constituency-building efforts will need to be part of the planning, implementation, interpretation, and analysis of local health status efforts.

Given the costs associated with ATOD problems, such community-based strategies will likely be a focal point of other prevention approaches in health care, generally. For example, the approach is finding support among those working with adolescents in pregnancy prevention, HIV-AIDS prevention, and violence prevention. ATOD prevention then becomes part of a broader definition of health. The net effect of this approach will be a broader constituency and resource base at the local level. As the nation focuses attention on access to care and the 37 million Americans without insurance, local data-gathering methodologies will play a key role in the community's capacity to redirect local resources to address this problem. The financing structures that may be put into place at the national and state levels may necessitate a more collaborative role among local providers of health and human services than any other time throughout the history of the United States. One key element that ATOD constituency-building groups can advocate for other health needs includes broader based prevention activities in the community problem solving mix.

The presence of African Americans, Hispanics and Latinos, Asian Americans, and Native Americans at the policy-making table is having a positive effect. According to the third year evaluation report of the Center for Substance Abuse Prevention (CSAP) of the Community Partnership Program, America's changing demographics have necessitated the improvement in traditional human services systems that have not been responsive to the needs of cultural minorities. Often, new technology is rejected foremost by those systems who have the most to gain from alternatives. CSAP's recent findings indicate that partnerships can reduce the number of drunk driving arrests, arrests for heroin possession, and markedly decrease narcotics cases in the court systems. Citations from the General Accounting Office (GAO) report of March 1993 show positive outcome results from the Gloucester Prevention Network, one of CSAP's original Community Partnership Programs.

Further evidence from the annual cross-site evaluations of the 253 community partnerships further elaborate on the methods of involving community representatives in meaningful policy development and decision-making. These results confirm the findings in a special issue of *Health Education Research* (September 1993) in which the coalition model is discussed among researchers in ATOD prevention partnerships as well as other health behaviors.

According to Keith Tones, in his editorial "Radicalism and the Ideology of Health Education" (*Health Education Research,* v. 8, no. 2, June 1993), the task facing health activists or educators is tackling the inequalities inherent in the consortium of big government and big business and the community. How does one take on the dominant ideologies? Communities are learning the skills necessary to challenge the existing power structures and to plan coherent solutions to the conditions under which the community alone is affected. Anything short of this approach is indulging in empty rhetoric.

Just as America is changing rapidly in its demographics, partnership communities are tremendously diverse and share similar economic and social problems. During the first two years, the typical partnership is a dynamic entity given to changing political tensions and priorities. The goal of the program is to shift the power base to the community in a shared responsibility between staff (who implement the strategies set by the governing structure) and boards. Over time, leadership and policy making tends to move more towards the community away from professional staff, from a staff-driven program to a grassroots-driven process. The planning of partnerships is strategic, based upon planning which takes into account two tracks; one track is engaged in immediate activities designed to demonstrate to the community that something concrete is underway, while simultaneously making long-term plans and connecting the emerging needs of the community with activity. Interaction among members of these coalitions increases proportionately to the diversity of its members. More ethnic representation predicts degree of internal communication. The members of the coalitions view the partnership as positive as well as their effect.

Findings are inconclusive as to whether too much diversity can have a negative effect. However, more diversity requires a longer time for consensus and interaction. Groups who have not previously interacted need to experience resolution of issues and problems and build together a history of collaboration. CSAP has found this time to be much longer than originally anticipated. Often, groups experience great disharmony and require intensive technical assistance and facilitation. Partnerships have been known to be very rocky at times, resulting in bad press, staff and board resignations. In many cases, the programs that fell to the lowest ebb in early developmental stages have emerged more solid than those with a more positive public image but lacking a deeper commitment to making a lasting impact. All, from one time to another, have thus experienced the accompanying emotional charges of both negative and positive ions.

The community as a whole learns, in this process, the skills of decision-making, community planning and evaluation, program development, and political dynamics. A new generation of grassroots leaders are evident in the hundreds of community partnerships in cities and rural communities across the nation. A new sense of urgency and energy has been recognized. Cultural subgroups previously uninvolved are now on equal footing with the dominant cultural groups and are encouraged by this open system approach to ATOD prevention.

Politically, partnerships have broadened to include issues around adolescent tobacco use, violence, HIV-AIDS, child abuse and neglect, and teen pregnancy. If the coalitions are truly engaged in preventing root causes, the risk factors are similar to many of the aforementioned health and social service problems. All certainly have strong correlation to ATOD problems as well (Cook, Roehl, Oro and Trudeau, in press). Central to the successful implementation of community partnerships, as CSAP is studying, is the dynamics of participatory decision-making. Consensus building, especially among people of diverse ethnic and cultural backgrounds, has been found to be consistently associated with the achievement of intermediate outcomes. Cooperation and participatory decision-making, for example, is a strong predictor of the achievement of partnership goals in the community and the ability to generate additional resources to combat drug abuse. Partnerships that become "problem-solvers" create a positive mind set in the community that the problems exist, have both short- and long-term solutions, and can be overcome. Members of the partnerships represent the diversity of the community, engage in consensus-building, and move on to create reductions in actual ATOD abuse behaviors such as needle use, alcohol-related car crashes, emergency room visits for drug use, etc. Another example of an intermediate outcome is the creation of community policing strategies. Community policing has been tried for a number of years and has improved community and police relations, providing intervention in domestic disputes, drug crimes, and neighborhood vandalism. Norms are set and reinforced which have contributed to lower costs for arrests, incarceration, treatment, and violence.

Yet, the law enforcement field itself, in many cases, has been the system most resistant to this approach. Once the community began to pressure law enforcement agencies to give greater internal support to the expansion of community policing, the approach received greater support. The community is changing the way police work is done by demanding a role in monitoring their own streets cooperatively. This approach engages the police as partners in problem-solving rather than as a public servant who is called upon to "do for" the citizen. In many ways, this is radically different from the policing approaches of the past.

This is an example of infrastructure changes which are often low cost, involve the community as volunteers, and shift more responsibility to the citizens in a partnership mode rather than a services provision mode. Community partnerships and community policing are similar methodologies and work well together in a complementary way.

Partnership models, such as those reported by the Midwestern Prevention Project (funded by the National Institute on Drug Abuse with additional resources provided by the Center for Substance Abuse Prevention) show an increase in policy-related activity in the second stage of development. After the community coalition has developed a sound infrastructure (bringing community agencies and grassroots representatives to the policy arena), can it move into the stage of making systems changes in the community? The research indicates that the partnerships begin then to capitalize on their status and positive regard to influence stakeholders. This combination of "roots and suits" is the essence of the coalition approach. While this is a new field which is only evolving in its technology, it is a challenge to traditional models of program evaluation. Preliminary findings indicate that it may not even be possible to disaggregate the combined effects of the individual programmatic component parts of a comprehensive coalition-driven program. The process of separating out the effects from the impact of the whole seems to be almost impossible. This model is revealing weaknesses in the scientific process as it applies to a unit of change, such as a community, where the whole is often greater than the sum of its parts (Gerstein and Green, 1993).

Indicators show a decreased use of alcohol, tobacco, and other drugs by school age children in the control community. Consistently, as each level or layer of activity is added to the intervention, the results improve exponentially. Further, the Midwestern Prevention Project has demonstrated that theoretical models with a combination of bottom-up and top-down organizational structures also show high generalizability and cultural adaptation. Other models generated from research-based models have low generalizability and low cultural adaptation.

Government and Philanthropy as Partners in Promoting Community Action: Building a National Infrastructure for ATOD Prevention

The concept of community mobilization is not a new approach to the elimination of community health problems. In 1979, The Surgeon General of the United States called attention to the substantial, unrecognized resources of the community for disease prevention and health promotion. *The Surgeon General's Report to The Nation* (1979) places the responsibility for health upon: (1) the individual, (2) the family for its members, (3) the health institutions for prevention, (4) the schools for the education, (5) business and labor for the worksite, (6) communities for health promotion, and (7) the government at all levels (U.S. Department of Health, 1979). This landmark document has given local organizers for health issues the opportunity to build community-based coalitions of interest on various health issues like drug and alcohol prevention (Stunkard, Felix and Cohen, 1985). It also opened the door by which many states and the federal government have provided seed monies for the establishment of these constituency-building efforts. This local constituency-building for ATOD issues has become one of the most promising approaches, stemming from the early work of the education of communities in their struggle to jointly face the consequences of ATOD issues (Butterfoss, Goodman and Wandersman, 1993).

Public pressure has been necessary to put into place policies that produce lasting behavioral change. The most obvious example is the movement to curtail drunk and drugged driving led by the Mothers Against Drunk Driving (MADD) which heightened community awareness and concern, monitored the judicial system to ensure consistency in the enforcement of existing laws, and promoted prevention and intervention programs in the schools, health care facilities, and government.

In 1977, the adoption of the Declaration of Alma Ata by the World Health Organization (WHO) was a milestone in the Health for All Movement launched by the World Health Assembly. The Alma Ata Declaration emphasizes three health principles: the involvement of the community, cooperation among different sectors of society, and the call for primary health care (WHO, 1978). Building upon these principles, a decade later in 1986, Canada's Ottawa Charter for health promotion identified five health promotion action areas: (1) building healthy public policy, (2) creating supportive environments, (3) developing personal skills, (4) strengthening community action and (5) reorienting community health services (Health and Welfare Canada, 1986).

The linkage of the prevention of alcohol, tobacco, and other drug problems to community action is timely because the field of community development, since the 1960s, has become a discipline with a body of knowledge and scientific methods that can be used for the prevention of ATOD. In the 1960s, community organization for social action was demonstrated to be effective in many realms from race to feminist issues. When congress funded the Economic Development Act in 1964, community organization advanced on the street and in the academe. In the late 70s and early 80s, several community-based health promotion efforts aimed at reducing the incidence of coronary heart disease and stroke were initiated in North Karilia (Finland), California, Minnesota, Rhode Island, and Pennsylvania. These efforts combined the practices of community organization and health promotion with an emphasis on citizen involvement to produce individual and environmental changes. The evaluation of the North Karilia project showed a significant reduction in three coronary risk factors and the tangible effects of a comprehensive, community based approach (Puska, Nissinen, Salonen, and Tuomileheto, 1983). *Healthy People 2000*, a blueprint for the nation's health goals, included alcohol and other drug problem prevention indicators. Community-based methods are fundamental to this approach. Public policy, individual approaches, and system change are encouraged in this document (U.S. Department of Health and Human Services, 1991). (See appendix for definitions.)

In an attempt to mobilize communities in the prevention of alcohol and other drug problems in 1988, the Center for Substance Abuse Prevention (CSAP), of the Substance Abuse and Mental Health Services Administration, Department of Health and Human Services, developed the Community Partnership Program. This model is comprised of 252 original sites at an annual budget of approximately $95 million for a five-year period beginning in 1990. An additional 20 coalitions were added in September 1994 for a five-year period as well. The magnitude of this program is unprecedented as a federally-funded community demonstration program for the prevention of alcohol, tobacco, and other drug problems.

The Community Partnership Program represents a most diverse and varied local-based constituency building family of projects in rural, suburban, and city environments. Budgets range from $70,000 per year to $1.2 million. While primarily focused on developing community participation and infrastructure changes in the delivery of ATOD services, monies can also be used locally to leverage other resources through minigrants, and through the creation of prevention services aimed at risk factors. Often partnerships subcontract for programming in areas of unmet need. The goal of the program is to create diversification of funding in the community among the public/private and philanthropic sectors and better utilization of existing resources while mobilizing volunteers rather than professionals.

The partnership model is volunteer driven, not staff driven, is committed to the community defining its own problems and creating local solutions. Technical assistance and training opportunities are provided through a national network of providers funded by CSAP. CSAP uses a lead agency model at the local level. The lead agency can be a variety of organizations and institutions at the local level. The lead agency serves as the fiduciary agent and the sponsor for the coalition-building activities at the local level. Currently, lead agencies in the partnership program include local health agencies, educational institutions, drug and alcohol providers, local government, and community foundations, to name a few. CSAP's Community Partnership Program is designed to emphasize sound planning and quality implementation in all types of prevention services. The program also seeks to enhance the community's leadership potential through the identification, recruitment, and training of people in the prevention of ATOD issues. Another important aspect of CSAP's Community Partnership Program is evaluation. The national evaluation of the 250 partnerships serves several purposes. First, it will aid local effort as a program planning and management tool that can contribute to local capacity building. Second, it will give national policy-makers a base against which to determine the net effects of a grant making program that seeks to stimulate local, state, and national infrastructure building for ATOD prevention services. This investment in evaluation is a long-term venture that competes for valuable project time and funding at the local level. As the community partnerships have matured, the commitment to sound evaluation has deepened. Policy-makers claim evidence to their intuitive sense that the complex mechanism of a local-based constituency building approach with its potential to impact politically, socially, economically and on the health of the population as the community partnership seeks, will be supported with an open, honest evaluation design.

Findings Suggest Reductions in ATOD Use Can Reduce Health Care Costs, Crime, Drunk Driving Deaths and Other Indicators

Preliminary findings suggest that the partnerships have successfully integrated natural and established leaders in power sharing. A synergy has been created when policies have been both set and implemented through the group process involving people most directly affected by ATOD problems with local leaders. This interactive model is both "bottom-up" and "top-down." Critics of this approach opine that it takes much longer to produce this support and generate tangible results.

In Tacoma, Washington, the SAFE Streets partnership is responsible for closing over 350 drug dealing locations in the city. They have also recorded a decrease in use of beer by eleventh graders and tobacco use by all school age children. Minority statistics are also impressive, with increased reporting of "no use" by Latino youth and Asian/Pacific Islander youth. While the population has been increasing dramatically in recent years, the ability to decrease any drug related crime is quite encouraging.

Community Demonstrations Learn from Mistakes

However, evidence from failed efforts indicates without involvement, commitment, and ownership of people in a community, efforts may produce only a facade that is easily influenced from political entities with little or no understanding of the complexities of the ATOD problems (Green, 1986). Political influences are most apparent in city or county offices, particularly those of the mayor or county executive. While this prestige and visibility can be very helpful to the organizing efforts of a community partnership, it can also be a source of control and domination, historical problems, and decisions imposed from local political factions rather than community input, process, and long-term effect. Rural programs are also challenged by the status quo. Lead agencies can be inhibitors to the community process and may bring cumbersome finance policies face to face with creative grassroots program strategies.

Perhaps the richest source of learning from this demonstration program has been from the coalitions who have not been successful in becoming a true partnership and have difficulty showing ATOD prevention outcomes. For example, negative publicity generated from disgruntled staff at one site caused coalition partners to distance themselves from the effort. Coalitions in large urban areas report more difficulty in keeping up with ambitious plans and time commitments. Their likelihood of receiving personal satisfaction from the partnership activity is less than those in less populated areas. In one instance a partnership relinquished funding due to the rigorous evaluation design, finding it to be more manageable to continue the coalition without the complications of funding, reporting, etc. It would be interesting to collect additional data from that community to see if the coalition had any effect on alcohol, tobacco, and other drug indicators after retrenchment.

Data is currently being collected regarding outcome results from specific types of partnerships. Cross-site data collection is underway for years four and five. Early results find that large urban areas had the greatest challenge in developing a governance structure that was acceptable to grassroots, traditional agencies and the emerging systems. The task of keeping up with government reports and evaluations, while attending to participation on a number of work groups and training opportunities, was overwhelming to a few partnerships. One group in Connecticut withdrew from the program citing their preference for a locally-funded coalition (Prevention in Perspective, 1990).

Policy-makers in government must come to accept and support the concept that infrastructure building at all levels of American society is a labor-intensive effort that is a long-term results-oriented approach and not a quick fix. Programs at the national, state, and local levels have a tendency to expect assumptions which are universal; they often assume that outcome results will be forthcoming after only a year or two of implementation. Such programs built on community needs and resources are not constructed through a set philosophy, methodology, or program design in a prescriptive fashion. Therefore, the model further complicates evaluation efforts. Community-driven programs do not fit the traditional molds created for research models which have clearer boundaries on the intervention and conditions for implementation. Community programs take a minimum of two years to develop and are just beginning to evolve into the appropriate prevention intervention stage. This process is dynamic and time consuming, somewhat like a moving target.

Community empowerment programs are not easily fit into existing program structures at any level. Policies must be in place at all levels of society that support local initiatives through funding, training, technical assistance, information sharing, networking, and evaluation. Perhaps this method was born out of frustration, lack of resources, and immediacy. The paradox is that if we can reconcile the questions of what can work, how it can work, where, and by whom, there must be an acknowledgement of necessary time and funds. One of the future policy challenges will be to create a national commitment to these approaches in light of increasing budget deficits.

Dr. Lee Brown, Director of the Office for National Drug Control Policy has cited on numerous occasions the need for more demand reduction policies in addition to supply reduction strategies, which were more dominant in previous administrations. Dr. Brown recognizes the value in community empowerment strategies and has given political support to the community partnership program in the President's National Drug Control Strategy of 1994. Community partnerships are mentioned throughout the strategy and are encouraged even in the supply reduction section of the document as well as the demand reduction section.

Economics Will Dictate the Necessity of Private and Public Sector Collaboration: Politics Will Chart the Course of Action

The philanthropic sector of America has demonstrated leadership in advancing the concepts of community as the place of focus for problem solving for several decades. In the 1960s and 70s, the Ford Foundation helped to establish community development approaches for economic development, poverty, and housing issues. In the late 70s and early 80s,

The W.K. Kellogg and Henry J. Kaiser Family Foundation helped to establish community health promotion programs that focus on the prevention of coronary heart disease and stroke, cancer, adolescent pregnancy, alcohol and drug abuse, injury, and infant mortality (Tarlov, et al., 1987). These philanthropies provided seed monies for communities to organize coalitions of citizens that represented a cross-section of the population to solve local health and human service issues. The foundation's money would help to legitimize local efforts in most cases as the positive reputation of these philanthropies along with their money would often provide the incentive for people of different interests working together. Foundations carry prestige and an element of further credibility for grassroots models. In the case of evaluation, training, and technical assistance, the foundations prefer to play a brokering role in helping the community coalitions identify outside resources for training and technical assistance and evaluation. Because they often require high standards of evaluation, they demand results from community based efforts. Depending on the specifics of the particular grant program and the interest of the foundation, evaluation is managed differently. These and other foundations have a long history in the sponsorship of joint meetings with government and the private sector to help advance the notion of community problem solving as the most promising modality in preventing substance abuse problems.

In recent years unprecedented resources have been spent on the serious ATOD problems of our nation's young people. The federal government proposes to allocate $12.7 billion to ATOD issues in the 1995 fiscal year; about 32 percent targeted for drug treatment and prevention education. Major foundations gave $87 million to alcohol and drug abuse projects between 1983-1987, and the federal government spent more than $23 billion to combat drug abuse in the 1980s. The recent Robert Wood Johnson Foundation Program "Fighting Back" alone is funded at $26.4 million. It is important to assess the effectiveness and outcome of those efforts so that youth-serving organizations can focus their limited resources on the programs and methods that work best.

While the design differences between the Fighting Back Program and the Community Partnership Program are numerous, there is general consensus that the programs are compatible and mutually beneficial. When both programs exist within one community, it is ultimately the community itself that must effectively coordinate the funding and implementation plans to avoid overlap and unnecessary duplication. Inherent in the expansion of resources from both the public and private sectors is always the dilemma of multiple funding choices, accountability, and visible outcomes. Communities must appropriately meet the needs of their locality while adhering to the obligations required by the funding sources. While both programs, in this case the Fighting Back and the Community Partnership, are compatible models with similar processes and goals, the community can experience many potential detrimental effects. When powerful national organizations become partners in a local community, especially those of such complex nature as ATOD problems, there can be competition, turf battles, and dependency upon outsiders. Ironically, the problems are the same issues the community organization process is aimed to ameliorate.

One local project director likened it to a cactus plant that has been over-watered. This Community Partnership director said she hoped the communities could survive funding, albeit prevent the continued ravages of alcohol and drug problems. Communities which have mastered the skills of problem-solving, resource sharing, and constituency-building are surviving quite well and seeing the improvement in service delivery, expansion of programs for youth, while increasing local citizens involvement.

In communities where skillful grassroots work is underway, partnerships are applying this knowledge to conflict resolution and mediation, for example, in gang prevention and incidents of violence and racial tensions often associated with problems of alcohol and drug use. Some communities are just too overwhelmed with new funding sources and are learning to manage multiple levels of resources and accountability. As their level of sophistication improves, so will the capacity to attract diverse sources of funds, staff, and needed facilities. The presence of growth will always be accompanied by the presence of problems. The ability to solve problems and move on will be an important distinction between those groups who survive and those who do not.

To ameliorate the problems facing sites with multiple funding sources, CSAP and partner foundations held regular policy meetings which resulted in agreements to do joint site visits; recognize each others' evaluation designs; and encourage mutual invitations to workshops, training, and conferences. Additionally, CSAP provides an annual Funders Forum in regions of the country to introduce creative ways to fund substance abuse prevention through existing foundation priorities such as youth, education, community development, and poverty programs. Foundation representatives attend and contribute to the greater understanding of public and private partnerships.

Opinions, to date, suggest that in most cases this overlap can be parlayed into a positive opportunity for the local constituency building groups. This includes increased visibility for the local effort, media coverage, added intervention and treatment resources as well as primary prevention capabilities. Communities have greater access to a wide range of technical support when they receive funding from both government and the private sector.

As a result of these efforts and the desire to have the opportunity to gain from the experience and knowledge of the philanthropic and private sectors, CSAP implemented a National Foundation Initiative. The purpose of this initiative is to continue developing permanent resources and a national infrastructure that will support the long-term efforts of local constituency building for ATOD issues. The partnership has over 25 foundation participants that include private family foundations, corporate, community, and operating foundations. The goals include collaboration on programs of mutual interest and emphasis; sharing of knowledge from promising practices, evaluation studies, and practitioner wisdom; access to new and changing public/private resources; reduction of duplication; enhancement and strengthening of standards of practice; continuity for demonstrated successful programs; and leveraging of new resources and services using the best of government and the best of the private sector (CSAP, 1991). Although in its infancy, several meetings of this partnership have been held and, as a result, early indications suggest that there is promise for helping the various sectors move towards a better understanding of the type of contribution each can make toward bringing about community-based solutions to the ATOD problem. The partnership can use its information, resources, and its complimentary skills to advance a national network that can impact the vertical and horizontal levels of neighborhoods, cities, counties, states, and the nation. The partnership can help local constituency building efforts by formalizing resources, promoting healthy public policy, and providing a national network that continues to identify, recruit, train, and support local leaders in ATOD prevention.

Politics and Economics Make Partnering Imperative

Two national issues make this public/private/philanthropic partnership a timely opportunity. First, there is the nation's budget deficit. Local-constituency building, be it for ATOD problems, economic development, housing, education, HIV-AIDS, or any other health or human service issue is a labor-intensive, long-term approach that requires on-going financial and human support. Policy-makers have a tendency to look for short-term approaches to these problems. As in the deficit itself, there is no quick fix to solving these complex problems. However, there is promise that by applying approaches that seek local ownership and citizen involvement in long-term solutions, community by community these issues can be resolved.

Empowerment does not mean teaching communities how to access federal grants; empowerment means teaching communities how to be independent from the federal resources.

As budget deliberations begin to take place, this CSAP Foundation Initiative can help the policy-makers in three areas; (1) through the evaluation methodologies and over 275 community partnerships coalitions in place they can educate policy-makers about the long-term value that local-constituency building can play in solving complex health and human service issues; (2) expanding this partnership to include other federal agencies that are using similar approaches can help to reduce duplication, competition, and overlap that could define over time the appropriate roles that the various levels of government and its agencies play in supporting such efforts; and (3) it can serve as an example how the public/private and philanthropic sectors can have formalized relationships that serve each interest while contributing to America's broader interest.

The second area where this partnership can make a contribution is a supporting role in the nation's quest for a resolve to our health care crisis. As various models are being debated by policy-makers, i.e., pay or play, managed competition or single payer systems, it is very likely that all of these approaches will require local, state, and national measurements of a population's health status. This assessment process will offer the opportunity to monitor over time the efficacy of practices put in place to improve health status as well as access to health care. It will also move local communities toward making more informed resource allocation decisions based on the current needs of its population.

Summary

The challenges facing the nation's capacity to solve complicated health and human service issues become even more complex when viewed in the context of budget deficits, health care reform, lack of a national uniform policy for local-based constituency building, lack of coordination among funders, competition among providers of service, and a lack of ownership for issues by local citizens. The politics of special interest and the economics of a growing budget deficit will drive the policy process at the national level. The opportunity in this set of realities is for the nation to put into place a long-term investment in human capital by implementing a national program that will provide support and expansion of community based problem-solving efforts like CSAP's Community Partnership Program. Having local constituency-building groups come together and identify local health status, community values, available resources, polices that inhibit and enhance local solutions, prioritized action, implement responses, provide management, monitoring and evaluation, and develop local training and technical assistance systems, can drive the nation towards solving these complicated political, economic, social and health issues.

Therefore, given the positive experience of CSAP's Foundation Initiative, the authors recommend that a more formalized national public/private/philanthropic partnership be supported with mandates to plan, implement, and support local-based constituency-building groups towards a healthy America. This would require policies that would direct funding to re-orient education systems to help grow community problem-solvers. It would require policies to develop formalized training and technical assistance systems to support existing and new efforts of local constituency-building. It would require policies that support vertical and horizontal information and resource networks. This "National Partnership for a Healthy America" could serve neighborhoods, cities, counties, states, and the nation as a linkage to bottom-up and top-down constituency-building that could ultimately make for a national consensus on healthy public policy. It could help to place attention on issues and policy where they need to be focused, at the local level. It could help to over time serve as a catalyst for the integration of health and human services, with benefits of cost, efficiency and improved access for all citizens. Finally, "The Partnership for a Healthy America" would seek to identify, recruit, train, and support leaders in re-structuring America's health and human service infrastructure by interactive techniques instead of reactive ones. This approach builds upon the democratic principles of our nation and offers the most promise for long-term solutions to our domestic problems.

6

Ethnographic Research Methods for Multicultural Community Needs Assessment: A Systems Change Perspective

Kristi O'Dell and Edith M. Freeman, Ph.D.

The purpose of this article is to describe and to illustrate the use of ethnographic research methods in conducting community needs assessments, emphasizing the active involvement of residents in the process which can then lead to planning, and implementing systems change efforts. Current literature on community development acknowledges the importance of involving residents in this process, which is designed ultimately to enhance a client-centered program development and evaluation process for preventing or reducing substance abuse, violence, economic stagnation, and other community problems (Cunningham, 1993; Freeman and O'Dell, 1993; Hawkins and Catalano, 1992).

Community needs assessments may serve a variety of purposes including providing baseline data for program justification and development. Using ethnographic research methods for such assessments allows for the identification of existing strengths and resources in a community that can then be built upon. The process is empowering of community residents in that strengths and needs are identified and validated by the residents themselves at individual, organizational, community, and social systems levels. Such an approach encourages a breadth and depth of exploration not generally obtainable with less inclusive quantitative methods. The following summary highlights how the different qualitative, ethnographic methods can facilitate this type of in-depth exploration and the subsequent development of prevention programs that involve a systems change perspective.

Ethnographic Research Process and Methods

The Inclusive Research Process

Those who write about using the ethnographic research process emphasize the importance of using unstructured and open-ended interviewing and of involving community residents to identify potential participants in the sample. An implication of this type of research is the need for the active involvement of community residents in planning and carrying out research procedures such as interviewing and data analysis, particularly when the focus is on sensitive issues such as the problem of substance abuse. Spradley (1979) highlights the need to have participants describe a culture or cultural scene in their own terms. Further, it is important that the researcher "listen for" and capture the culture being described by participants and their diverse experiences with systems that impact their community and substance abuse problems, without changing the meaning and import of those descriptions. Involving residents in data analysis or in reacting to the researcher's conclusions can improve the cultural sensitivity of the analysis process, and, therefore, its accuracy.

Another element of the qualitative research process is to analyze the data collected through ethnographic methods. The value of using such methods is lost if quantitative analysis procedures are used (Patton, 1982). Hasselkus (1988) indicates that a content analysis of ethnographic data from a service program can be organized around themes of meaning, sources of tension, and relationships between clients and professionals. Additionally, the authors of this article identify a process of reflection and learning in action as ethnographic data are analyzed, rather than fitting the data into preconceived categories for analysis.

Hasselkus (1988) defines themes as the meaning which individuals assign to their daily living experiences and the patterns of informal learning embedded in that meaning. According to this author, meaning itself is derived from ". . . those values, beliefs, and principles that people use to organize their behavior and to interpret their experience" (1988: 686). Further, meaning should be understood within the context of the shared cultural meaning system and community norms about substance use, prevention, or violence that are found when the focus of study is a community and its residents as a collective. In this chapter's needs assessment research, the authors defined themes as underlying and sometimes unspoken meanings inferred from what a participant said or did in the interview or in an experience that is described during the interview.

Finally, study findings should be presented in a manner that is consistent with ethnographic methodology. Such studies seek to capture the unique life worlds of individuals (Spradley, 1979), to identify the personalized meanings embedded in each individual's experiences. While it is possible to identify collective reactions and experiences of study participants, the most valuable benefit of this method is identifying diverse, individually focused reactions that flow from, rather than are directed by, the research (McCracken, 1988). Therefore, the findings are often presented primarily in a case study format that contains the participants' actual language and perspectives in all their uniqueness, along with secondary summaries of key similarities found within the perspectives of the study sample as a whole.

The findings of the ethnographic research process are especially useful also for clarifying the generational issues across different ethnic groups in multi-cultural communities and within a particular ethnic group. Regarding the latter, the ethnographic study described later in this chapter includes the following reflective comment from an Hispanic member of a community with white, African-American, and Hispanic residents:

> ". . . You need to keep in mind that the community has a broad spectrum of Hispanics. . . . You have the second, third, and fourth generation Hispanics. They are gonna be carrying a lot of cargo with them; negative things about themselves and their culture . . . where they have been trying to straddle two worlds . . . thinking that they have to make choices . . when they really shouldn't have to . . . and then you got the people that just arrived yesterday and they're gonna have different . . . needs. The undocumented are looking for a place to hide first of all."

Ethnographic Research Methods

The culturally rich process described in the previous section is facilitated best through the use of research methods that encourage participants to draw upon their subjective impressions and indigenous status within a community. Ethnographic methods that can be used to conduct such research include key informant and snowball techniques wherein informal leaders and other key persons are asked to share their knowledge of the community and of individuals who "should" be interviewed. This type of convenience sampling helps to identify potential participants who represent different subgroups within an ethnic group as well as those from different ethnic groups (Freeman and O'Dell, 1993).

The ethnographic methods also include the community forum, unstructured individual interviews, focus groups, social indicators, rates under treatment (RUT), and on-site direct observations in a community. These methods have been described in detail elsewhere (Marshall and Rossman, 1989; Taylor and Bodgan, 1984; Freeman and Pennekamp, 1988), so only the four methods utilized by the current authors in their needs assessment research are discussed in this section. The four methods are community forums, multicultural social indicators, ethnographic interviews, and focus groups which provide the foundation for later program evaluation practice research (see Appendix B). By combining various data collection techniques, the limitations in one strategy can be compensated by the strengths of a complementary strategy.

Community forums (see Appendix B) involve public testimony and anecdotal experiences with open-ended questioning. Three such forums were held prior to using the other three methods in the current needs assessment in order to identify key informants and gather preliminary data about community needs. The sampling for community forums is purposeful with equal representation among different interest groups. Areas of diversity that are present in the community are well sampled in terms of age, racial/ethnic group, gender, socioeconomic status, occupation, and location within the community. The advantage of the community forum method includes opportunities for empowerment when the residents' views are solicited, listened to, and respected. Moreover, different factions within a community are allowed to discuss their similar and different views in a neutral territory (Freeman and Pennekamp, 1988). Disadvantages can include the airing of complaints as opposed to constructive feedback about needs and resources and the possibility that some less vocal or hopeful individuals (Marshall and Rossman, 1989) will not participate. Formal and informal community structures were used in the authors' research to encourage residents from a range of backgrounds to participate and to make the forums more systematic, comprehensive, and inclusive.

Individual Ethnographic Interviews (see Appendix B) allow the researcher to ask most of the questions in an open format, use repetition to clarify informants' responses, and encourage informants to expand their responses. In the authors' needs assessment, the researcher asked most of the questions in an open format, used repetition to clarify informants' responses, and encouraged informants to expand on their responses. There are three primary strengths in using ethnographic interviewing for community needs assessments that greatly enhanced the current research process. First, there are benefits from a face-to-face encounter with informants in their natural setting. These benefits may include facilitating cooperation among informants, facilitating access for immediate follow-up data collection for clarifications and omissions, obtaining data on non-verbal behavior and communication, and the opportunity to observe the physical and emotional climate of the community. Second, open-ended questioning facilitates the discovery of the informant's perspective of processes, of the nuances in culture, and of the complex interconnections in social relationships. Third, ethnographic interviewing facilitates analysis, validity checks, and triangulation of research methods (Marshall and Rossman, 1989).

Despite these potential benefits, much of the success of ethnographic interviewing is related to the knowledge, skill, and experience of the researcher. Researchers may impose their values and data may be subject to observer effects that are both obtrusive and reactive. Subject selection is another area of potential problems. If the selected subjects fail to represent the broadest range within and across cultures, the analysis is fundamentally flawed. If subjects are reluctant to talk freely or are less than truthful about their observations about problems and strengths in the community, the research is jeopardized. Recording equipment to gather data and computer equipment and programs to analyze data may be expensive. Finally, ethnographic interviewing is difficult to replicate if procedures are not explicit, and even then data obtained may be dependent on the researchers' opportunities or characteristics (Marshall and Rossman, 1989). Consistency in training the interviewers and frequent research team meetings were used to identify and resolve potential problems in this area in the authors' needs assessment research.

Focus Groups (see Appendix B) involve "bringing together groups of people to talk about their lives and experiences in free-flowing, open-ended discussions" (Taylor and Bogdan, 1984: 113). These group interviews are typically focused upon a single topic. There are several advantages to using focus groups for community needs assessments. They are a rich source of data that can be obtained in a short amount of time. The group composition can be varied, so that the perspectives of different populations within a community can be examined. The group interaction gives a feel for the range and diversity of perceptions and elicits issues that might not have emerged in individual interviews. Group interviews allow the researcher to observe how a group constructs and defines its reality. Focus groups lend themselves to replication, so that the thematic results from several focus groups can be compared. The potential problems of focus groups include the following: the possibility that the discussion may be dominated by a few people; individuals with different or unpopular views may fear group antagonism and hold back; and individuals who know one another may be constrained by past experiences with one another. The researcher's careful selection of participants and setting the ground rules at the beginning of the discussion can help to minimize these problems (Marshall and Rossman, 1989). These important guidelines were followed in the needs assessment research described in this chapter.

Finally, a community's *Multicultural Social Indicators* or resident demographics can be used to help increase understanding of the geographical, social, economic, political, and cultural climate of the area. Census tract data are a ready source of information classified by ethnicity and age and useful for the researchers' multicultural community. Census information includes the types of residential housing, educational attainment, type of employment, income, and typical family structures within a community. Other sources include city planning documents and legal, health, and business statistics on a community. Based on knowledge of these multiple methods, a needs assessment was conducted in a multicultural community experiencing substance abuse, violence, economic, and school dropout problems.

The Multicultural Community Needs Assessment: Methodology

Purpose of the Needs Assessment

The authors conducted the community ethnographic needs assessment as the result of a cooperative agreement between a Midwestern graduate school of social work and a private foundation. The purpose of the needs assessment was to explore how the community residents view their life circumstances and in what ways a private foundation could better serve community families with young children (the foundation was currently sponsoring several adolescent projects). The researchers selected an ethnographic research design for the study in recognition of the importance of the organizational and community context of the families' lives and to explore the major problems identified previously from the families' frames of reference. It was assumed that understanding their perspectives could help to identify community resources and systems change goals that could prevent or decrease the community's problems. The researchers explored the ideas of members of the community in four major areas of their lives through individual interviews and focus groups. Attention was given to both unique and common aspects of their perspectives. The four areas for individual resident interviews include the following:

1. definitions of the community where they live and/or work and the strengths, resources, and barriers within that community, especially barriers related to the community's efforts to address its problems;
2. their individual and familial strengths, talents, and resources;
3. what self-sufficiency and success mean to them; and
4. their concerns, needs, and personal obstacles related to a goal of self-sufficiency.

The primary topics addressed by the focus group portion of the study included the following:

1. the informal and formal organizations' purposes, priorities, roles, and nature of contacts with residents in the community;
2. their definition of the community and assessment of its strengths and needs;
3. their identification of important events and people, including leadership patterns within the community;
4. their definitions of self-sufficiency and the community's status and goals in this area from an organizational perspective; and
5. themes of meaning underlying these organizational views of the community and its residents.

The Two Samples

One hundred and ninety individuals participated in the study. Fifty were interviewed as individuals (34) or as couples (16), and the remainder (140) were interviewed in fourteen separate focus groups. Participants in individual interviews included any community resident who was pregnant or who had an infant up to 18 months of age. Included also were immediate and extended family members in the same household, such as the father of the children, and other persons identified as family members who might not have a blood relationship with the participant. The racial composition of this sample was representative of the community's overall racial composition: 75% Latino, 15% white, and 10% African-American.

This sample of 50 persons was selected through a snowball technique (Freeman and Pennekamp, 1988) in which potential participants were identified by key informants in the community including service providers, formal or informal community leaders, and knowledgeable residents. A staff member from the project made the initial contact with the key informants (some of whom were identified through the community forums), explained the purpose of the study, and solicited the names of potential participants. The staff member is a former resident of the community who maintained personal and professional ties in the community and was able to provide the researchers with a deep understanding of the community history.

The researchers attempted to include a cross section of residents who met the main criteria for inclusion in the primary sample. Other criteria were included to vary the characteristics of the sample and to reflect the make-up of the community itself (Taylor and Bogdan, 1984): age, gender, marital status, number and ages of children, type of housing (public or private, single family or multiple dwelling), and ethnic group. Among potential participants who were Hispanic or Latino, an attempt was made to include both first and second generation residents in the sample. Individual interviews were conducted with all participants in their homes or in the offices of community organizations and agencies as determined by each participant for his or her comfort and convenience.

A second sample in the study included groups and individuals representing twelve community organizations and six areas of special interest in the community. The number of participants in the focus groups ranged from three to fifteen. The project's staff person and key informants helped to identify organizations and individuals that represented the various racial, age, political, and socioeconomic segments of the community. Overall, in spite of efforts to recruit a racially diverse sample of focus group participants, there was insufficient representation of African-Americans in this sub-sample (less than 5 percent). To insure a broad sample of special interests, participants represented the following categories: education and employment, political influence, economic and business, arts and recreation, housing, legal, the media, culture, religion, and social services including health. Some of the natural leaders and organizations included in the sub-sample fit into more than one of these categories. The focus groups were held in the offices of organizations participating in the session or in some other site selected by the organization. Both individual interviews and focus groups averaged one and one-half to two hours in length.

The Setting

The community of 4,126 persons is located in a Midwestern metropolitan area of approximately 500,000 residents. In terms of geography, the community is bounded by streets on two borders and by railroad tracks and river bluffs on the other two borders. It was settled originally in the early 1800s by European immigrants. Many of these original families eventually moved away and in the early 1900s Latinos began to move in due to a rapid increase in available work with the railroads. Latinos later lived predominantly in the central part of the area.

African-American families began moving into the area just prior to the Civil War, and into public housing in the 1960s when those developments were opened. These public housing developments were racially-mixed initially, but gradually one in particular has had predominantly African-American residents during recent years. In the 1990s, with the exception of public housing, African-Americans live mostly in the south part of the area where some of those families settled originally.

As noted previously, Caucasians have lived in the area continuously since the early 1800s, mostly in the west part of the area. Members of these three racial groups live and interact together in some ways, for example, in terms of housing and cultural events, but they remain separate in other areas of their lives, for example, in their social relationships. Yet, members of this community seem to experience more tolerance and harmony among themselves than groups in other parts of the city, with persons from all races being viewed as "outsiders" until they indicate a willingness to accept and become a part of the community.

Building Initial Rapport and Relationships

The researchers met with the project staff member prior to data collection over a period of 2 months focusing on issues of trust, communication, and cooperation with one another toward developing and implementing the project. As was mentioned before, the staff member is a former resident of the community who maintained personal and professional ties in the community. He has an interest in the welfare of the community and is respected in the community. He provided initial access to community organization members for the community forum, individual interviews, and focus group participation. The project staff member met with potential participants, reviewed the study purpose, and obtained their verbal agreements to participate. He then introduced the interviewers to the participants to establish the initial trust necessary for the interviews. This process is useful in gaining access to and establishing rapport with the community and organizational leadership and with the individual participants. The community had negative experiences with researchers previously who misrepresented their goals in obtaining information about the community and its residents. Consequently, members of the community were reluctant to participate in research projects. Potential participants were assured that participation in the needs assessment was voluntary and that those individuals who chose not to participate would not be penalized in any way.

Ethnographic Procedures

Community forums were held by the researchers to gather preliminary data about the community, as noted previously. The three forums were advertised through posters displayed in community centers and through announcements in an area newspaper. The forums were held in three different community sites to encourage the broadest multicultural participation. Potential key informants were identified among the participants for later recruitment of volunteers for the interviews and focus groups. In addition, multi-cultural social indicators data were obtained from the most recent area census profile, the state employment office, and the city planning commission.

The researchers conducted individual interviews and focus groups simultaneously over a period of four months. The authors selected interviews as one of the research methods as the research goals were relatively clear and well-defined and due to time constraints (Taylor and Bogdan, 1984). These interviews allowed the researchers to obtain a large amount of data quickly, a wide variety of information from a large number of subjects, and allowed for immediate follow-up questions and interviews as needed with some participants. A potential limitation of interviews without participant observation is that distortions in data are more likely, as interviewers may interject personal biases (Marshall and Rossman, 1989). Interviewer training, rehearsal, and on-going feedback were used to reduce the possibility of interviewer bias in this project.

The principle investigator, an experienced focus group facilitator, and the research assistant facilitated the focus groups. Focus groups were selected as another research method to gather a broader range of ideas about the needs and strengths of the community and to allow members of the groups to reflect together and individually on the ideas being discussed (Schon, 1983). The group interaction gave a feel for the range and diversity of perceptions, and helped to identify issues which might not have emerged in individual interviews, such as concerns about city policy makers who ignored the special needs of the community and problems with youth gangs, drug abuse, and family violence. The latter problem, in particular, was only spoken about in focus groups (Taylor and Bogdan, 1984). The potential problems among focus group members that were previously described were minimized with careful selection of participants and by laying down ground rules with each focus group. Individual and organizational participants were paid a nominal fee for their participation.

Study Instruments

The interviewers used two separate instruments to explore the views of the two samples of participants. The researchers designed an interview guide for conducting the individual interviews with residents and with representatives of the media, churches, and small business merchants in the community. The purpose of this type of interview guide is to get as close as possible to the people and situations being studied by "following" the participant's lead (McCracken, 1988). This interview guide served to remind the interviewer to ask about certain topics. In the current team research, the guide provided a way of ensuring that all the interviewers were exploring the same general areas with participants (Patton, 1980). In funded research and qualitative evaluation the guide can be used to give sponsors a sense of what the researcher will actually cover with informants, as was true in this research project (Taylor and Bogdan, 1984). The guide was open-ended in format, consistent with the goal of ethnographic research (Spradley, 1979). The use of an interview guide presupposes a certain degree of knowledge about the people one intends to study and so is useful, as it was in this situation, where the researcher had already learned something about the participants through fieldwork, preliminary interviews (Taylor and Bogdan, 1984), and community forums. The guide consisted of a set of nine topic areas, representing an expansion of the four areas noted previously. The actual topics covered during interviews were determined by the direction that each participant took as the interview unfolded.

The researchers designed a second interview guide for use with community and service organizations during focus group sessions. This guide was also open-ended in format with examples of topic areas that were both similar to and different from those contained in the interview guide for individuals. All individual interviews and focus groups were audiotape recorded to facilitate accurate transcription of the sessions.

The researchers pre-tested the interview guides with community volunteers to identify any problems in using them to collect data and then revised them as needed (three individual participants and one community organization were part of this pre-test phase). Faculty of the school of social work, the interviewers, and staff of the project, before and during the pre-tests, reviewed the instruments and other research materials. Their suggestions along with the results of the pre-tests were used in making revisions of the instruments. Involving the interviewers in providing this feedback became an integral part of their training for the study.

Training of the Interviewers

The principal investigator selected three interviewers based on their research and practice experience and skills in interviewing. The principal investigator trained the interviewers, who were two doctoral and one master's level social workers, in four two-hour sessions. A tour of the community provided an orientation to the history and present circumstances of the community. The principle investigator then conducted sessions introducing the interviewers to the instruments, consent forms, reference articles, and procedures to be followed. Additionally, the interviewers were instructed on the purpose, content, and process of ethnographic interviewing.

During the training sessions, interviewers analyzed the interaction in two pre-test interviews conducted by the research assistant, based on what they had learned about ethnographic interviewing. Interviewers also participated in simulated, video-taped interviews that were used during training to help them evaluate their own skills in ethnographic interviewing. They then individually developed a plan for improving their interview skills. Interviewers, for the most part, conducted interviews with participants of the same racial background as themselves, white, Latino, or African-American to increase cultural sensitivity and understanding of participants' responses. It was hoped that such assignments would bridge social distance and cultural differences between each interviewer and participant.

Data Analysis

The principal investigator and the research assistant were responsible for the on-going data analysis with input from one of the key informants as previously described. This input helped in interpreting cultural issues related to the data. To facilitate data analysis and assure confidentiality, each interview and focus group was assigned a code number based on a system developed before the study. The audio-tapes were transcribed into verbatim written narratives. A format was developed to allow the researchers to make notes directly onto the transcripts as a first step in identifying and noting relevant data in each interview. This preliminary informal review of the first written transcripts made it possible to identify particular content categories and themes that seemed to be common across interviews and focus groups, an important step in this type of research (Hasselkus, 1988; and McCracken, 1988). Two separate data coding sheets were developed to include different content categories for individual interviews and focus groups. A second step involved transferring or coding the researchers' notes and other data from each transcript onto individual and focus group data coding sheets.

Validity and Reliability

Checks on the dependability of coding procedures by co-researchers and participants, and clearly describing the research procedures and the rationale for any modifications enhanced the reliability of methods. The replicability of findings in this study are enhanced by using a triangulation of methods. Keeping all collected data in well-organized, retrievable form, for example, as in a computer, makes them available if the findings are challenged or if another researcher wants to reanalyze the data. Research exhaustion and saturation were not threats to this short-term study, however, the fact that the community has been studied by other researchers could have limited community participation, but it did not in this situation. Finally, the definitions of the primary constructs of community and self-sufficiency may be specific to the point in time when this study was conducted and to the present community (Marshall and Rossman, 1989).

Findings Related to the Types of Ethnographic Methods Used

Community Forums

There were five primary insights obtained from the community forums that had implications for the changes that were needed within and outside of the community:

1. Many different community services would be needed due to the different subgroups, i.e., ethnic, intergenerational, socioeconomic, including prevention and treatment.
2. The high school dropout rate in the area was attributed to not having a high school located in the community.
3. There was lack of responsiveness to community needs by the school board and other large systems outside the community.
4. There were conflicts over informal and formal community leaders, e.g., who should be acknowledged, who should make decisions, what types of prevention services were needed, if and how youth should be involved in community changes.
5. There was mistrust of researchers due to past experiences with researchers, e.g., lack of feedback and credibility by past researchers.

Multi-cultural Social Indicators

Indicators Related to Residents

The tri-ethnic makeup of the community was one of its strengths. This aspect of cultural richness was a factor in how the community was viewed by the larger metropolitan area. Outsiders, as well as insiders, appreciated the culturally-oriented library, newspaper, restaurants, and churches. Latino music, crafts, and other aspects of the culture were a magnet for visitors to the community during ethnic celebrations as well as at other times. Thus, the unique culture of the community was viewed as an important strength. Thirty-seven percent of the population was white, 19 percent was African-American, and 43 percent were other races with less than 1 percent either Native American or Asian/Pacific Islander. Eighty-six percent of this population was classified as minority (non-white and/or Latino), while 67 percent of the residents were Latino (of any race). Because Latino individuals can choose how they are designated racially, these figures do not total 100 percent. This made it difficult to obtain an accurate count of the number of Latinos in the area.

Educational attainment was another important characteristic considered in understanding the community. Among community residents 25 years and older, 67 percent did not complete high school, while 33 percent were high school graduates. Approximately 12 percent of residents had one or more years of college. These generally low levels of educational attainment had an impact, no doubt, on several indices of the quality of life for many area residents, for example, employment, income, and housing.

Most families lived in owner occupied, single family dwellings (71 percent), that were built before 1950 (66 percent) and which were valued at less than $19,999 (81 percent). The average monthly rent paid for rental units was $82.00. The vacancy rate in the area was 19 percent, down 5 percent from the prior census. One strength was that the majority of these households consisted of families (76 percent) which included married couples with children (50 percent of the families), while only 16 percent were single female householders with children. These figures on family constellation indicate the possibility of multiple unmet needs for many residents coupled with decreasing financial resources based on unemployment rates.

According to the state office of employment security, unemployment for the area averaged 9.5 percent for the year 1990. The largest percent of employed residents worked in the occupational field of manufacturing as operators, fabricators, and laborers (38 percent). The second highest concentration for residents was in technical, sales, and administrative support occupations (21 percent). Forecasts of employment indicated that the number of manufacturing jobs would decrease due to the national recession and the influx of products from foreign manufacturers. Service and retail jobs were expected to increase within this community, similar to trends at the national level and in some other communities in the greater metropolitan area. While these trends may affect many segments of the community negatively, they may have a greater effect on those more vulnerable to changes in the labor market: the young, unskilled persons, non-English speaking persons, and ethnic segments with the highest unemployment rates currently, African-American and Latino residents.

In terms of income, another index of quality of life, 77 percent of the employed residents earned less than $19,999 per year. Moreover, 21 percent of all households received some form of public assistance. Thirty-three percent of the residents were below the poverty line of $12,700 income per year for a family of four. In terms of ethnicity, 26 percent of Caucasians in the area had incomes of less than $12,700 per year, as did 75 percent of African-Americans, and 24 percent of Latinos. Seventeen percent of persons 65 and older also were below the poverty line at that time.

Indicators Related to Social Service and Community Organizations

Many current social service and community organizations have been part of the area for periods ranging from seventeen years to over one hundred years, another unique strength of the area. Social service and community organizations include a Latino-oriented social service agency, a primary care health clinic, and a counseling and recreation center. A housing organization began as a grassroots community organization initiated by residents. Its members have been able to form valuable coalitions with other community, city, state, and federal organizations. This rich history, along with these organizations' records of service, contributes to the high visibility and acceptance levels of these organizations by many community residents.

These organizations have served a rapidly changing community which seems to be in transition in a number of important ways. For instance, the population has declined by nearly three times since 1960 with future population estimates expected to continue to decrease through the year 2000. Thirty-four percent of the population was 0-17 years of age with Latino and African-American families having a greater percent of children under 17 years than white families proportionately.

It is clear from the multi-cultural social indicators that this community has many strengths. Due to those strengths, many community members continue to choose to reside in the community and visitors continue to patronize cultural businesses and organizations in the area. Also evident, however, is that the community has a variety of needs including affordable housing, educational and vocational training programs, and employment with improved income opportunities. A large number of the families have children, indicating the potential for a repeated cycle of early dropouts from school, under- or unemployment and involvement in youth gangs, community violence patterned after family violence, substance abuse, and early parenthood (Kane, 1987).

Ethnographic Interviews

The definitions of their community extend beyond geographic perimeters to include certain aspects of community residents themselves, such as, race and ethnicity, longevity in the community, and perceived strengths and needs of individuals and the community. Many participants define the community in terms of the tensions among long time community members and new move-ins who are the perceived source of undesirable changes in the community. These newer members of the community are viewed by some of the other residents as being different in their life styles and values. Such tensions are evident in the following vignettes:

> ". . . a lot of new people I see coming to this area are the upper middle class and us that been here all our lives are lower and middle class people. They're trying to come in and take it over and everybody feels eventually that's what's gonna happen . . . now we're all gonna end up getting pushed out maybe . . ."
>
> "From Sacred Heart to over here, everybody's lived here for a long time. . . . You can see, I live down the street from a big park. I know a couple of years back . . . kids could go out and play as much as they want, walk anywhere around here . . . not now that they have the so-called gangs running around here and some people from the projects down there.

There are also tensions within the Hispanic community related to unanticipated needs and concerns of residents about power inequities among them:

> [From a Latino woman] ". . . there are Mexicans and there are Mexicans. . . . It's who you know when it comes to getting information . . ."

Despite such tensions, some community residents note times when different groups worked together toward a common purpose of impacting systems outside the community, such as the school district:

> "When the community has to get together, you know they'll get behind one another whether they have differences or something as long as they all believe in one thing . . ."

Other examples of community action or systems change provided by residents during interviews include getting the city to reconsider a decision to rezone a street for business and planning how to get a political organization to support a community resident running for and winning public office.

Focus Group Sessions

As with individual participants, focus group participants define the community in a number of ways including: geographically, both as the physical area and in relation to the greater city area; racially and culturally, in terms of closeness and sources of tension among residents; and regarding hopes for the community in the future. With regard to the latter:

> "The families here, if they can make a decent living, a living to sustain their families, they want to stay here . . . they want a better community."

Some focus group participants are less optimistic about the future of the community as a residential community due to the power of encroaching external business interest:

> ". . . commercial property, it's becoming very valuable, nobody cared for it before except us, now everybody cares for it . . . what I'm worried about is that when we do the development that we don't knock out the people that have lived here . . . 'cause we still want to maintain the community . . ."

Some Latino participants talk about the community in terms of it being a center of the city's Latino culture and the potential for further development culturally.

> ". . . we all have the same culture here . . . we have the same language, very similar beliefs . . ."

A Systems Change Perspective 93

> ". . . We would like to be an attraction that people come to share our culture with us . . . by no means do we want to be exploited. . . . We're just as American as anybody else, and that's what we want to bring forward."

Despite statements of cultural unity, there is also a theme about the unique problems of multiple generations within the Latino community:

> ". . . You need to keep in mind that the community has a broad spectrum of Latinos . . . you have the second, third, and fourth generation Latinos, and then you got the people that just arrived yesterday and they are going to have different . . . needs . . ."
>
> ". . . The newly immigrating families tend to be much more . . . compliant with traditional values, less likely to get into drug or school problems. But the second generation it just, falls apart . . ."
>
> ". . . it's just so hard for us to get work for them [undocumented] anymore . . . that causes friction not only amongst the non-Latino community but as well as within our own Latino community . . ."

The organizational representatives participating in the focus groups identified a number of important strengths and resources related to the community (an alternative school and a church for example:

> "Our goal was to serve thirty kids for the year. Well, we've exceeded that. . . . We're serving kids that are gang members, that are teen pregnant moms, that have limited English proficiency. Yet at this school, we have a zero dropout rate. But, we're just, you know, a drop in the bucket . . . thinking of the services that are needed here or that need to be expanded."
>
> "The _____ Church is . . . involved in the community for a long time . . . several pastors have made it a real point of trying to identify the needs of the community and doing some outreach activities recently with homeless . . . other churches are involved too."

The needs, gaps in resources, and problems noted by the focus group participants include a broad range of issues from infant day care, inadequate housing, job training for special groups including older teenagers and adult males, bilingual education, increasing rates of teenage pregnancy, job discrimination, low self-esteem, lack of political power in the community, substance abuse, and school drop-outs.

> ". . . a lot of families . . . if one sister gets pregnant and then the other sister will . . . I work with one family where the three sisters are all at home and they all have children and they're teenagers. They are already expecting their eleven year old [sister] to have a baby. She feels left out because I'm talking to the sisters . . ."
>
> "In one training program, to get employed during the summer, kids had to go through eight weeks without getting paid . . . there wasn't money for that time. . . . They were going to have to wait that long before they could even get a job. So, sometimes the motivation was not there."

Many of the themes identified from the focus groups are similar to the themes identified by individual residents, but there tended to be more emphasis by organizational representatives on the themes of a loss of control and power than in the individual interviews. The coalitions and clubs tended to discuss these themes and those related to community pride and leadership more than did the other organizations. In contrast, education and social service organizations focused more on the multi-generational theme of value conflicts and school dropouts. Differences between findings for individuals and for organizations included their priorities in terms of needs and problems, in what community strengths were identified, and in how self-sufficiency and collective empowerment were defined.

Implications for Systems Change Efforts

This ethnographic needs assessment of a multicultural community revealed a complex set of views, strengths, and problems, as well as a community that is segmented and in transition. Some of this complexity was obvious before the study began. Much of it, however, became more apparent as the different layers of residents' experiences unfolded;

underlying themes emerged, residents' meanings were shared, and interpretations were made as the data analysis progressed. A number of implications flow from the findings that resulted from this data analysis process.

First, it is clear that if they are conducted effectively, as inclusive community-involved processes, needs assessments have strong political ramifications. Encouraging a community to assess its strengths, sources of power, and barriers to further empowerment and community control is a consciousness-raising process. Residents are asked to reflect on the connections between their personal problems and the social conditions within and outside of the community that help to maintain those problems (Guiterrez and Ortega, 1991). As in the current research, they also identify their common experiences with disempowerment and begin to speculate on common social or political action strategies for changing systems that caused those experiences (Freire, 1989). In a sense, the needs assessment process validates community members' reactions by providing a venue for their voices which have previously been unacknowledged and unheard. Researchers need to be aware of these political ramifications and to help study participants anticipate and understand the emotional and cognitive reactions they might have as a result of the needs assessment process.

Secondly, this needs assessment has highlighted the diversity among the voices within the community as is expected when using the identified ethnographic methods. An on-going mechanism for community planning is needed to continuously reassess and consider the different needs of the various subgroups. Such a mechanism is important for the type of consensus building that is necessary for collective political action and structural change at the large systems level (Yeich and Levine, 1992). For example, most groups in this community have a common concern about youth gangs, school dropouts, early parenthood, and substance abuse. These youth-related issues may be potentially an area of consensus because they seem to be the community's highest priority. On the other hand, different perspectives about community leaders, homelessness, intergenerational value conflicts, and encroaching business interests may indicate areas that will be difficult for consensus building initially.

A third implication is the need for continued cultural sensitivity as part of this community's planning and implementation of systems change strategies based on the needs assessment. The four ethnographic methods used in this research were especially appropriate for insuring an inclusive, culturally sensitive process. In this community, and in similar ethnic communities, it is important to maintain the use of such methods for influencing *and* evaluating the systems change implementation process. Once prevention programs are developed to further implement systems changes, similar culturally sensitive program evaluation methods should be used (see Appendix B). This requirement is important whether prevention programs are focused on drug, violence, school dropout, or pregnancy prevention. Efforts may focus on policy changes (reducing the availability of alcohol and other drugs or guns to youth) or on other systems changes (getting a community resident on the school board as a first step in making the board more responsive to the community's special needs).

Finally, an important implication of the study findings is the need to use multiple systems change strategies combined with micro strategies. The systems change strategies necessary in the current community range from power analyses which involve assessing who benefits or suffers if certain social conditions remain the same, sources of personal or political power in the community, and barriers to collective empowerment (Guiterrez and Ortega, 1991) to grant writing (see Appendix C). These macro strategies designed for systems change are more effective when they are used in combination with various micro strategies as shown in Appendix C, and when they are integrated with the ethnographic research methods described in previous sections. Many communities, including the one focused on in this needs assessment, have existing skills and resources related to these combined strategies. The process during and after the needs assessment should identify and build on a community's existing strengths related to systems change, as well as help to develop new skills.

Conclusion

The multicultural community needs assessment illustrates how ethnographic research methods can be used to better understand the complexity of residents' experiences, strengths, and needs as dynamic individuals, families, organizations, and communities within the larger social systems. This approach is time intensive and expensive, but given sufficient time and funding, other potential problems, such as reliability and validity of methods, can be minimized with triangulation of methods, careful description of and rationale for selection of methods, and sufficiently trained interviewers or observers.

It is through the process of mutual exploration of community resources and needs by researchers and residents that the next step of appropriate and effective program development can be taken. Programming that is designed to better serve this or similarly complex communities will need to be equally complex and multilayered. This multilayered approach is consistent with using a combination of macro and micro strategies to accomplish systems change.

7

Fighting Back (Project Neighborhood) and Systems Change

Keith Brown, B.A.

Alcohol, tobacco, and other drugs (ATOD) abuse is America's number one health problem, responsible for half a million preventable deaths annually. The morbidity and mortality from ATOD use and abuse are staggering, as are the direct and indirect costs to society. These costs include violence, crime, overburdened human service systems, reduced industrial productivity, and higher health care costs. ATOD abuse touches every aspect of the American society, and ways are needed to reduce its toll.

As a health care philanthropy, the mission of the Robert Wood Johnson Foundation is to improve the health of the American people. One of the Foundation's four major grant making goals is to promote health and prevent disease by reducing the harm caused by alcohol, tobacco, and illegal drugs. Thus, in February 1989, the Robert Wood Johnson Foundation embarked on the Fighting Back Initiative. Its mission was stated as follows:

> *Fighting Back projects are community-wide coalitions designed to reduce the use and abuse of alcohol and illegal drugs by consolidating existing resources into a more accessible system of care. This comprehensive system includes: prevention, early identification, treatment, aftercare services, relapse prevention and neighborhood improvements.*

Fourteen cities, including Kansas City, Missouri, were funded by the Foundation and it currently supports all of them. It also supports a

Fighting Back National Program Office (NPO) which is based at Vanderbilt University in Nashville, Tennessee. The NPO provides ongoing program oversight and technical assistance to the community-based projects.

The Kansas City Fighting Back (Project Neighborhood—PNH) was started in March 1992, following a short period of planning. The mission of Project Neighborhood was consistent with that of the Foundation:

> *To reduce the harms associated with substance abuse by consolidating existing programs and resources into a community-wide system of prevention, early identification, treatment, aftercare services, relapse prevention, and environmental improvements. With everyone's involvement, we increase partnerships through* **Collaboration in Action.**

Before PNH in Kansas City
- The drug problem was considered largely the responsibility of the law enforcement and judicial sector of the community.
- The sale of alcohol to minors was a common practice.
- There was a tendency of public authorities to turn their backs on the problem out of frustration, especially after it became clear how limited they were in controlling usage and promoting demand reduction.
- Treatment Centers had largely been co-opted to the law enforcement model, with most of their referrals mandated by the courts. Treatment beds were very limited; thus creating a situation that made it virtually impossible for a large number of clients to receive inpatient treatment.
- There existed a fragmentation of resources to cohesively address the problem.
- Churches, neighborhood organizations, small businesses, and individual residents in the core community had little or no involvement in substance abuse demand reduction.
- Based on community needs assessment during PNH Planning period (1990-1992) the following statements were developed:
Drugs have unleashed massive destruction in Kansas City, particularly the urban core community. There is less concurrence and understanding about steps that should be taken to resist the ready availability and excessive abuse of Alcohol, Tobacco, and Other Drugs in Kansas City and the region as a whole.

Social Indicators

The data reported for the State of Missouri, Jackson County, and Kansas City was collected by Catherine Heimovics (1993) of the University of Missouri in Kansas City, Missouri. The information presented here was designed to serve as a baseline set of data which can be used to assess community-wide impact of Project Neighborhood, along with its collaborating partners, in efforts to reduce the use and abuse of ATOD in Kansas City.

The data was organized into the following clusters: (A) General Mortality Indicators; (B) Alcohol and Drug Use Indicators, (C) Communicable Disease Indicators; (D) Other Indicators; and, (E) Treatment Indicators. The data was reviewed by several individuals who were knowledgeable about community health and alcohol and drug issues in Kansas City, and their observations are included in the following discussion.

A. General Mortality Indicators

1. *Mortality Rate: All Causes of Death*
   The trends evidence a consistent rate with very little fluctuation. Throughout the period, however, Kansas City had higher rates of death than either the county or the state, with just one slight decrease from 1991-1993. Jackson County and the State of Missouri experienced a slight increase from 1992-1993.

2. *Homicide and Suicide Mortality Rate*
   Trends indicate relative consistency in the death rate with some slight decreases and increases. Kansas City remains higher than the state and county, but in 1993 there was a decrease in the death rate. Jackson County also experienced a slight decrease at that time. Offered as an explanation for relative stability over time of these rates, community leaders discussed the possibility that the effort to separate real felons from drug dealers has affected trend lines. All community leaders expressed interest in seeing these rates presented by age.

3. *Motor Vehicle Accident-Related Mortality Rate*
   As evidenced by trend lines from 1987-1993, all categories appear relatively constant. Jackson County, from 1988 to 1991

What Have We Accomplished to Date?
Project Neighborhood, Inc., Impact on Systems Change at a Glance

Programmatic Areas	Before PNH	Accomplishments 4 years after PNH
Alcohol Public Policy	• Ineffective underage liquor sale law enforcement • Underage liquor sales • 2,167 licensed accounts	• Community Covenant to reduce liquor sales to minors • 7.8% decline in sale of beer • Decrease in liquor outlets • 1,401 licensed accounts
Media Relations/ Public Awareness	• Under-reporting • Marketing without measurement • PA on the back burner • Lack of focus	• Over 200 documented print media in 1995 • Social marketing • Center piece of PNH • Focused
Treatment Referral/ Relapse Prevention	• Uncoordinated treatment community • 30 day to 90 day waiting list • No treatment follow-up	• Treatment contracts with treatment providers • 48 hours to 4 days residential bed availability • Developed case management follow-up model • COMBAT Central Referral System
Project SAVE	• Denial of ATOD in Faith Community • Rejection of scientific approaches to prevention • Lack of involvement	• 25 churches involved in prevention TOT • General acceptance of scientific approaches to prevention and continuum of care • Active involvement
Community Mobilization	• Environmental high risk factors • Limited Community Leadership in ATOD • About 2-300 drug houses • Lack of ATOD evaluation • Competing and incoherent prevention activities	• Significantly improved environments • Community capacity building/Community involvement • Sixty percent reduction of drug houses • Outcome-based evaluation • Collaboration/team work and linkages
Community Policing	• Traditional policing • Centralized services • Poor community/police relations • High crime rate	• Community-based policing • Decentralized services, e.g., CAN Centers • Improved community/police relations • Reduce crime rate by 24 percent

experienced a slight increase in motor vehicle-related accident rates, yet continued to remain below rates for Kansas City and Missouri. Kansas City experienced a decrease in 1991, but an upward movement is seen in 1992. It could be that the relative stability over time could be the result of widespread use of seat belts. However, this would be one indicator that would need to be looked at by age group to obtain a more accurate mortality rate.

4. *Non-Motor Vehicle Accident-Related Mortality Rate*
Trends from 1987-1993 evidence a gradual decrease over time in the non-motor vehicle accident mortality rate. In 1990-1991 there appears to be an increase of deaths, and in 1991-1993 a slight decrease. The state and county remain consistent with each other, yet the county continues to be below the state.

B. Alcohol and Drug Indicators

5. *Substance Abuse-Induced Mortality Rate*
All these alcohol and drug induced causes of death were further combined into one category, All Substance Abuse-Induced Mortality Rate.

Trends from 1987-1993 indicate that the state has remained constant in the substance abuse-induced mortality rate. The county has experienced some fluctuations, while showing a dramatic decrease in death rates from 1991-1993. According to persons familiar with the anti-drug tax initiative, county trend lines may reflect effort since 1991 to enforce and prosecute drug dealers. Kansas City has remained comparable to state rates until 1991, when rates remarkably increased. From 1991-1993 there have been slight decreases.

6. *Alcohol Dependence Mortality Rate*
The trend fluctuated between 1987-1990, with Kansas City and Jackson County increasing in 1991, while the state, overall, evidenced very little change in 1991. State, county, and city show declines between 1991 and 1993. Kansas City remains higher than county or state, however. Given a somewhat older

state population, recalculation of rates for at risk age groups has been suggested as supplemental information.

7. *Chronic Liver Disease/Cirrhosis Mortality Rates*
   Trends from 1987-1993 indicate some stability in rates. In 1990, Kansas City experienced a decrease and leveling-off period until 1992. However, in 1993 all three categories have experienced a slight increase.

8. *Alcohol-Induced Deaths*
   The causes of death considered to be directly caused by alcohol. They were reported separately under this combined heading:

   Alcohol psychoses
   Alcohol dependence syndrome
   Non-dependent abuse of alcohol
   Alcohol polyneuropathy
   Alcohol cardiomyopathy
   Alcoholic gastritis
   Chronic liver disease and cirrhosis, alcoholic
   Excessive blood level of alcohol
   Accidental poisoning by alcohol

   Trends indicate that from the years 1987-1989 the city, county, and state had comparable rates of alcohol-induced deaths. In 1990, Kansas City experienced a significant decrease in death rates. In 1991, the city experienced a noteworthy elevated rate. In 1992-1993, slightly decreased.

9. *Drug-Induced Deaths*
   The causes of death considered to be directly caused by drugs. They were reported separately and under this combined heading:

   Drug psychoses
   Drug dependence
   Non-dependent use of drugs (excluding alcohol and tobacco)
   Accidental poisoning by drugs
   Suicide by drugs
   Homicide for poisoning by drugs
   Undetermined (a/s/h) for poisoning by drugs

Trends from 1987-1993 indicate that Missouri has not been entirely stable, but relatively consistent, whereas the Jackson County and Kansas City rates have consistently fluctuated over time. Kansas City experienced higher rates of drug induced deaths than Jackson County and Missouri until 1990. In 1990, the city remained comparable to the county rates until 1993, and at that time experienced a decrease in the drug-induced death rate. Kansas City's rate remained below the death rates for both Jackson County and the state of Missouri. Decreases in city and county rates may reflect county-wide efforts to arrest drug dealers.

10. *Severe Alcohol-Related Crash Rate*
    Trends for all three categories indicate some consistency in severe alcohol-related crash rates. Over time, Kansas City's rate has experienced fluctuations, but decreased for 1990-1992 and appears to have leveled off. Age breakdowns will be completed to provide more information on variations within the population in the PNH target area.

11. *DUI Rates (Driving Under the Influence of Alcohol)*
    For the years 1987-1989, the state experienced slight decreases and increases. From 1990-1992, the state evidenced a consistent leveling-off in DUI arrest rates. From 1987-1992, the county experienced gradual increases in its DUI arrest rates. Kansas City's rate has fluctuated over time; however, in 1991-1992 there appeared to be a slight decrease. To further understand these fluctuations, community leaders thought it would be best to aggregate this data by age, race, and sex.

12. *Liquor Law Offense Arrest Rate*
    For the years 1987-1992, data was only available for the city and for the state of Missouri. Both Kansas City and the state experienced major increases in arrest rates; in Kansas City the rate peaks in 1989 and the state rate peaks in 1990. Both show decreasing rates for 1991 and 1992; arrest rates are lower in 1992 than in 1987.

13. *Disorderly Conduct Arrest Rate*
    In 1987 the disorderly conduct arrest rate in Kansas City was four times the rate for the state. The state has increased slightly from 1987-1992, while Kansas City's rate is a little more than two and a half times that of Missouri. Since this rate represents administrative response to behavior as much as it does the behavior itself, national numbers and figures for St. Louis may provide better context for understanding Kansas City trends.

C. **Communicable Disease Indicators**

14. *Incidence of Gonorrhea and Syphilis*
    Trends for 1987-1989 indicate a steady decline of rates in Kansas City. From 1989-1991 there appeared to be a steady decline and level-off until 1992. The years 1992-1993 saw a dramatic decline in rates. County and state rates continued steadily across the board with no real dramatic fluctuations. Kansas City rates remained higher than the state and county until the 1992 decline. Jackson County information is exclusive of Kansas City.

    Trends from 1987-1990 indicate the incidence of syphilis to be sporadic over the 1987-1993 period. From 1990-1991, there was a remarkable jump in rates of incidence with leveling out from 1991-1992, and a notable decrease from 1992-1993. Rates in Jackson County and the state remained consistent until 1990. From 1990-1993, there is an increase in the county rate, while the state remains constant. Kansas City had a higher rate of incidence throughout the period from 1987-1993. Jackson County information is exclusive of Kansas City.

    Offered as an explanation for the behavior of these diseases in Kansas City were situational events occurring from 1987-1989. According to Health Department sources, during that time, drug dealers from out of the country brought to Kansas City a strain of gonorrhea which became rampant. Much attention was paid by the health professionals to get control of this disease, and less attention was paid to syphilis, henceforth the 1989-1991 increase in syphilis and the 1989-1991 decrease in gonorrhea incidence.

15. *Reported HIV Cases*
    Trends from 1987-1990 indicate an overall increase in rates. From 1990-1993 the overall state of Missouri appeared to experience continued heightened rates at gradual intervals. Jackson County, from 1989-1991, experienced some decreases in rates of HIV infection incidence. From 1991-1993, the county experienced gradual levels of increases with some leveling off. Kansas City, from 1987-1990, experienced increases in rates with some leveling off during that period. From 1990-1992, Kansas City's HIV infection rate gradually decreased, and from 1992-1993 leveled off. Community leaders expressed a need for data to include existing cases, as well as a need to look at AIDS related deaths.

D. **Other Indicators**

16. *Larceny/Theft Offense Rate*
    Trends from 1987-1992 indicate an overall consistent trend line for all three categories. However, Kansas City from 1989-1992 appeared to evidence a slight decrease over time.

17. *Burglary Offense Rate*
    Trends indicate from 1987-1992 a consistent pattern of Burglary Offense Rate among Jackson County and the state of Missouri. Burglary offense rates within Kansas City slightly decreased from 1987-1990. From 1990-1992, Kansas City experienced a gradual increase in burglary offense rates with some leveling off.
    There is widespread belief that theft and burglary reflect the need for money to support drug habits. Obtaining data at a smaller level (perhaps by zip code) might show more variability in these indicators than overall rates suggest. Aggregating this data would allow for a comparison of the PNH target area and the rest of the city.

E. **Treatment Indicators**

18. *State-Supported Substance Abuse Admissions Rate*
    Admission data for state-supported treatment admissions were not available for Jackson County and Kansas City for two years prior

to 1992. Selected admission data for new admissions were those people who had not previously sought treatment. Selected admission data was not available prior to the year 1992 for the whole state of Missouri, Jackson County, or Kansas City. This was due to a computer system used by the state of Missouri Department of Mental Health which made data impossible to retrieve. The waiting list for admission to inpatient treatment took between 30 days and 90 days.

19. *State-Supported Substance Selected (New) Admissions Rates*
Missouri state information was available from 1990-1993. Trends for the state indicate a decline in new admissions rates from 1990-1992. The years 1992-1993 evidenced a leveling off period. Jackson County and Kansas City both showed a rate of increase of new admissions from 1992-1993.

Target Area Description

Geographic Location
The physical area covered by PNH is large and reflects the sprawling character of the greater Kansas City metropolitan community. The target area encompasses some 55 square miles and is bounded north to south by the Missouri River and 63rd Streets, and by State Line and I-435 on the west and east, respectively. The population of the target area was approximately 195,000 in 1990.

While the Project covers one-sixth of Kansas City, it serves as a microcosm of the city. Most of the major public institutions are housed within the target area's boundaries. The project area includes Kansas City's poorest neighborhoods and highest crime areas. All of the city's public housing and most of the community's ethnic enclaves are also located there. It serves as the home of business, banking, and professional activities. The majority of professional headquarters are located there. With all of these elements coexisting there, the area enjoys the interest and commitment of the community's leadership.

The target area is served by the Kansas City, Missouri School District and most of the District's facilities are located within these boundaries. A number of the metro area's major corporations have headquarters within the Project's boundaries. Seven of eleven of the major medical institutions, all four of the publicly supported health clinics and all ten of the publicly supported alcohol and drug treatment centers are located within the target area.

Population

The 1990 population in the PNH target area was 195,000. This represents a sharp population loss for the target area over the last twenty years. The city as a whole, in contrast, lost about 4 percent of its population between 1980-1990. Relatively modest decreases are forecast by the regional planning agency over the next twenty years; it is projected that the area will contain about 174,000 people in 2010.

Minority Groups

The target area has traditionally been home to the minority communities of Kansas City. Between 1980 and 1990, African Americans became the largest single group of the area's population, accounting in 1990 for 49 percent of the population. When combined with other minority groups, non-whites became the majority in 1990, 56 percent of the total population. Persons of Spanish origin comprise 6 percent of the population.

Housing

The housing stock is relatively old; a little over half of the housing in 1980 was single family, and over half was built before 1940. From 1970 to 1980 there was a 14 percent loss of units, and availability of housing is a continuing problem for residents of the target area. It is estimated by housing officials that another 8-10 percent of the total units were lost between 1980-1990. One indication of the poor fit between the housing market and the target population is that there are 2,000 families (largely from the PNH area) on the waiting list for Section 8 housing, while 500 families await openings in conventional public housing. Kansas City is one of the ten most segregated communities in the country in terms of housing. Eighty percent of the 130,000 African Americans who live in Kansas City, Missouri, reside in the target area.

Education

Housing patterns are amplified in the makeup of the student population of the Kansas City, Missouri Public School District. With a total population of slightly more than 30,000 students, approximately 70 percent are minorities. The school district is in the midst of a court-ordered desegregation plan which entails a massive reorganization of the school district, including the busing of 80 percent of the students from neighborhood schools to a network of magnet schools.

Of equal concern is the dropout pattern in the Kansas City district. The 1990 Superintendent's Task Force on Dropouts in the Kansas City School District found that approximately half of the students admitted to the district do not complete requirements for graduation.

Employment and Jobs

School drop-outs do not automatically become employed youths. Within the target area, young African American males have also dropped out of the labor market in significant numbers. Almost one-half of the 18-19 year old black males are jobless, compared to 30 percent for white males in the same age group. Among 16-17 year old males, only 25 percent of African Americans are employed, compared with nearly 50 percent of white youth.

Business

The target area is the center of commerce and industry in Kansas City. Of the 100 largest companies, banks, and professional organizations that comprise the Civic Council, 90 percent have their headquarters in the target area. The Vice-President of the Civic Council is on the PNH Board, as is the president of the metropolitan Chamber of Commerce.

Income

The target area includes a mix of lower, middle, and upper income households. Minority households, as a group, have significantly lower purchasing power than do white households. Nationally, 40 percent of African Americans earn under $10,000 per year. In contrast, only 10 percent of white Americans report earnings under $10,000. A more telling statistic, and one which is available locally, concerns public assistance. In the service area for PNH, nearly 19,000 African American children receive some type of public assistance to meet their daily survival needs. Public assistance programs include: food stamps, school meals, Medicaid, public housing and/or cash assistance.

Crime

According to statistics prepared by the Kansas City Police Department, this area is the most violence-prone in the city. In 1990 it had 60 percent of the murders, 50 percent of rape arrests, and 41 percent of armed robbery arrests. In the 27 categories of offenses for which the Police Department is responsible, the arrest rate in this patrol division was disproportionate to the population residing there.

The Ad Hoc Group Against Crime and the Police Department jointly monitor activity associated with drug sales. Both sources estimate that there are between 200-250 drug houses operating in the target area at any given point in time.

Government

The PNH target area includes all, or portions of, four of the six Kansas City councilmanic districts and is also a significant portion of Jackson County, Missouri. Using Jackson County boundaries as a guide, there are 59 elective offices within the county. Of these, half are held by individuals who reside in the target community. Of the latter, 66 percent of the elected officials are minorities. Prominent among these is Emmanuel Cleaver, elected Mayor of Kansas City in April 1991 by 58 percent of Kansas City voters. He was recently re-elected in 1994.

Neighborhoods

Unlike some cities, Kansas City has a tradition of viable neighborhood organizations that date to the post-Pendergast reform years of the 1940s. The Project area is broken into some 79 distinct neighborhoods, although the degree to which they have active organizations varies.

Project Neighborhood has been described by many in Kansas City as the organization that has achieved the most impact while maintaining the highest level of input from residents in the fight against the devastation of substance abuse. There are numerous areas where Kansas City has noted PNH's value to the community. This chapter focuses ignificant positive systems changes accomplished as a result of the implementation of PNH's six major areas of emphasis: (1) Alcohol Public Policy, (2) Media Relations/Public Awareness, (3) Treatment Referral/Relapse Prevention, (4) Project SAVE, (5) Community Mobilization, and (6) Community Policing.

Since PNH in Kansas City: Specific Programmatic Outcomes

Alcohol Public Policy

Project Neighborhood's work in public policy is particularly interesting in the Kansas City market. With Missouri being the corporate location for Anheuser-Busch, most attempts at legislation regarding alcohol have been ineffective. Project Neighborhood has chosen to work on the local level, both with government and beyond government to the wholesalers and distributors at the retail level.

In the winter of 1995, PNH achieved a high point in both alcohol public policy and public awareness. After months of community meetings, community leaders, liquor control officials, law enforcement professionals, and a cadre of reporters watched as sixteen liquor store owners signed a Community Covenant. This document went far beyond what the owners were required by law to do. Before signing the Covenant, the owners had been the target of sting operations for sales to minors; most had at some time been charged with sales to minors. Since the signing, the operations continue and not a single Community Covenant location has been cited for sales to minors. The locations display fetal alcohol warning posters, no trespassing signs, and no loitering signs. As one owner said, "As long as Project Neighborhood calls, I'll be here . . . for as long as it takes to clean up my corner."

The local Anheuser-Busch wholesaler also participates in the discussion regarding alcohol sales to minors. He provided Project Neighborhood with sales records from the six-month period immediately following the Covenant signing. Those records show a 7.8 percent decline in sales of beer—the alcoholic beverage of choice among underage drinkers. It was his interpretation of this data that PNH had indeed stemmed the tide of underage sales in these locations, both through heightened awareness of the owners and heightened awareness of the underage drinkers that you can no longer buy alcohol in stores which signed the Community Covenant. From 1989 to 1995, there has been an overall decrease in the number of liquor outlets in Kansas City. According to Miller Highlife sales, there were 2,167 licensed accounts in 1989. By May of 1995, that number had declined to 1,401, or 766 fewer outlets: A drop of over 35 percent. Prior to PNH's involvement, few showed concern for the concentration of liquor licenses in this area. As the result of early intervention from Project Neighborhood and the subsequent mobilization of the community, a major drug store chain's request for a liquor license was denied. Residents are now notified by the liquor control board anytime a license is requested within their community. In a memo to Dr. Len Saxe of the Brandeis National Evaluation Team, Greg Dixon of Fighting Back said, "The beer wholesalers are using this data to persuade the city and county that they are being damaged by Project Neighborhood." The entire Covenant process was captured in the documentary, *Community Covenant, Collaboration in Action.*

City council members have taken up the fight on ordinances suggested by Project Neighborhood regarding open containers and chilled 40 oz. beverages, along with existing legislation limiting liquor licenses and strengthening enforcement of other current laws surrounding alcohol abuse issues. A preliminary evaluation report following the first six months of operation reveals dramatic changes in the areas covered by the Covenant as compared to the control group areas. Law enforcement officers and neighborhood residents have observed a significant reduction of risk factors and activities associated with alcohol and drug abuse in the participating communities. On the other hand, the control group areas have not changed; in fact, in many respects these areas are experiencing more problems associated with alcohol and drugs than ever before.

Media Relations/Public Awareness

The public awareness component is interwoven throughout all of the programming of Project Neighborhood. Not only do people have to learn about the program, they must be able to understand and utilize it once they do discover the program. Activity is viewed not only from an outcome evaluation standpoint, but also from an image perspective. The activity must fit the defined image of Project Neighborhood if the community at large is to understand the complicated nature of the organization.

Media relations for Project Neighborhood have always been good in Kansas City. The executive director is well known by longtime reporters and was frequently called upon to comment on various substance abuse related issues. There were, however, several other organizations that were viewed as the "experts" in the substance abuse field. More often than not, they were called upon first.

Over the past 18 months, Project Neighborhood has thrown major resources to the area of media relations. The communications manager, a former radio news director, has created a relationship with the working media which has led Project Neighborhood to be know as *the* expert in the field of substance abuse in Kansas City. On a weekly basis, reporters will contact Project Neighborhood for resource information on stories. They recognize Project Neighborhood will pass along knowledge without requiring attribution—they often provide it anyway. This, along with being very selective about media events, allows Project Neighborhood to generate media almost at will. A major change has been the ability of PNH to influence more coverage of substance abuse issues than ever before. It has also changed the traditional approach of public awareness to the use of social marketing.

Treatment Referral/Relapse Prevention

One of the strongest aspects of the work of Project Neighborhood is helping those who are ready to enter treatment for a substance abuse problem get into a treatment program in a timely manner. Project Neighborhood's treatment referral component has cut the time-frame from assessment to actually receiving treatment by over 75 percent. Support for the individual does not end there. PNH provides comprehensive case management and relapse prevention support through a variety of activities:

1. Development of job skills which gives someone in recovery a way to move forward with life.
2. A social services linkage which allows them to access available service industry supports.
3. Community reintegration skills training to help them adjust to a life of sobriety.
4. Relapse prevention support within the community through Project Neighborhood mobilizers.

Project Neighborhood's Treatment committee meets monthly and offers various treatment providers the opportunity to learn about programs which Project Neighborhood and other agencies are offering to help the human service industry maximize its delivery in the area of substance abuse treatment. Today, COMBAT has developed a central referral system. The treatment community has organized itself rather than remaining fragmented.

Project SAVE (Spiritual Advocacy for Value Exchange)

Project SAVE is a creative, community-church endeavor spearheaded by the Kansas City Globe Newspaper in collaboration with Project Neighborhood, Inc. (The Robert Wood Johnson Foundation, Fighting Back). Its purpose is to develop and implement strategies for preventing and/or reducing substance abuse in the Greater Kansas City African American faith community. The project provides Christian educational opportunities for preventing substance abuse. Participants are church leaders who play pivotal roles for catalyzing the ecumenical community in the prevention and/or reduction of substance abuse in the interfaith community.

The idea of Project SAVE was conceived by the *Kansas City Globe* editor and publisher, Marion Jordon, along with his wife and managing editor, Denise. They took their idea to Keith Brown, executive director of Project Neighborhood, and later the two organizations teamed up to make Project SAVE a reality ("Training Underway for Area Churches," *Kansas City Globe,* Dec. 8, 1995-Dec. 14, 1995).

Project SAVE is an interfaith anti-drug abuse prevention program designed to reach youth ages 6-12 and is infused into the weekly Sunday School curriculum. Over 25 churches have been recruited to participate in the project.

Participating churches engage the Sunday School Superintendent or Director of Christian Education into the program and they are responsible for completing four, six hour training modules.

According to Rev. Jim Bridgeford, Interfaith Program Coordinator, "There's not a week that goes by where somebody in the congregation is not directly or indirectly impacted by a family member involved with substance abuse."

The curriculum was developed by Dr. Jacob Gordon (1995), Professor, Kansas University. Dr. Edith Freeman, Professor, Kansas University, is responsible for monitoring and evaluating the program.

Recruitment

Active recruitment for project participants began in August 1995. An initial letter was sent to participants containing an abstract of the project, and requesting them to recommend a representative from their churches. The Faith Community Coordinator (Rev. Jim Bridgeford) followed-up with phone calls and personal visits with the church leaders. The first

Indicators for Success: Project SAVE

1. Increases in awareness and knowledge of substance abuse.
2. Behavioral changes.
3. Evidence of curriculum infusion into Sunday School lessons.
4. Evidence of infusion of substance abuse issues into the teaching, preaching and discussion aspects of congregational programs.
5. Anti-substance abuse message on church bulletin boards.
6. A special church event on substance abuse issues.
7. Evidence of family commitment to ATOD no-use policy.
8. Evidence of church members' involvement in community prevention efforts.

---

phase of the process focused on recruiting twenty-five (25) leaders from among the "Top Fifty Gospel Preachers."

Generally, leaders were highly responsive and thought Project SAVE was long overdue. Leaders perceived the project as providing the required "tools" for helping them implement drug awareness and anti-drug education in their Sunday School curriculum for children aged 6-12 years.

Ministers expressed no trepidation about the challenges the project would present. Issues that surfaced concerning dogma and creed were minute. A spirit of healthy competition appeared as ministers committed themselves to launching Project SAVE in their own respective churches.

Orientation Session

On Monday, September 25, 1995, twenty-five (25) ministers convened at Project Neighborhood for an orientation session along with the Director of Project Neighborhood and the Project SAVE staff. Discussion centered on logistics and programmatic issues, and a sense of urgency was expressed by all present. The leaders vowed their support to the purpose of the project. The vast bulk of the session revolved around concerns about the length of time required for training, the requisite number of training sessions and appropriate church staff members to participate in the project. Ministers were also interested in developing on-going drug prevention programs and generating funds to help sustain the project.

Pilot Projects: Mariah Walker AME Church and Mt. Pleasant Baptist Church.

Two churches consented to participate in a pilot project and provide feedback relative to the curriculum and implementation process. On September 30, 1995, 9:00 a.m.-12:00 noon, a training session was held at Mt. Pleasant Baptist Church (Rev. Louis Bell, Pastor). Staff members from Mariah Walker AME Church (Rev. Sandra McFadden-Weaver, Pastor) participated in this activity. Approximately thirty (30) people attended the session.

The pre/post tests and evaluation were thought to be valid and reliable instruments of assessment. Recommendations from this session were as follows:

1. Utilize videos and other multi-media sources appropriate to adult learning styles.
2. Content was relevant to understanding "street drugs" terminology.
3. Every member of the congregation should be exposed to the curriculum content.
4. Ministers should receive training regarding spirituality and substance abuse prevention via an "integrative approach" to changes in perception of the drug abuse epidemic in the African-American Faith Community.
5. Follow-up training for in-service church-staff development.

Training of Trainers (TOT)

The methodology for training consisted of having the Sunday School Superintendent or Director of Christian Education attend four weekly sessions from 9:00 a.m.-4:00 p.m. at Project Neighborhood. At the conclusion of the training cycle, participants received a certificate. If a session was missed, the trainee was expected to receive the content at the next training cycle for that particular module. With the certificate, the church staff member will return to his/her church and train others, and incorporate this religious based substance abuse curriculum into the church's Sunday School lessons. The project has received certification from the Missouri Substance Abuse Counselor's Certification Board, Inc. Graduates from this project will receive twenty-two(22) contact hours.

Initially, trainees expressed concern about the contents being Biblically based. After an in-depth explanation and a request by the Project Coordinator that they bring their Bibles to the sessions, trainees were more receptive and fervid in their participation. Small group activity and other interaction exercises facilitated the training process as well as group solidarity.

Evaluation

The results of the first regular trainee group are summarized below:

• **Modules I and II: *Definition of Terms and The Role of the Black Church in Human Services***
Knowledge Questions: Trainers showed a positive increase in knowledge after the training workshop. The trainers demonstrated at least a 90 percent increase in knowledge in the positive direction.
Attitude Questions: Overall, attitudes changed in the positive direction. However, trainers' attitudes for question 7 (Christian education can be used to help black youth and families develop positively without including curricula on community issues such as substance or violence prevention) changed in the negative direction.

• **Modules III and IV: *Effects of Substance Abuse and Circle of Wholeness***
Knowledge Questions: Overall, trainers positively increased their knowledge after training. However, for question 3 (alcohol has many serious consequences for communities and society; as many as 50 percent of all hospital admissions are alcohol-related) the trainers showed a negative increase in knowledge.
Attitude Questions: Trainers' attitudes changed positively, except for attitudes about question 5 (it is unrealistic to expect that many children and youth will abstain from using substances because they are exposed to negative community conditions) which changed negatively.

• **Module V: *Spirituality and the Recovery Process***
Knowledge Questions: Trainers showed a positive increase in knowledge. Increase in knowledge improved at least 80 percent after training.
Attitude Questions: Trainers' attitudes changed in a positive direction. Attitudes changed positively at least 90 percent after the training workshop.

- *Modules VI, VII, and VIII: Scientific and Traditional Substance Abuse Prevention, Program Evaluation, and Resources After Training*
Knowledge Questions: Trainers demonstrated an increase in knowledge in the positive direction. Trainers showed at least a 75 percent positive increase in knowledge after training.
Attitude Questions: Trainers' attitudes changed in a positive direction. Trainers demonstrated at least a 64 percent positive change in attitude after training.
TOT Attendance: The overall trainees' attendance was very high, 89.5 percent. The attendance for Session 1 (Modules I and II) 100 percent; Session 2 (Modules III and IV) 75 percent; Session 3 (Module V) 83 percent; Session 4 (Modules VI, VII, and VIII) 100 percent.
Future Directions: All future activities will focus on implementation of ongoing Project SAVE activities and church representation on Project Neighborhood's prevention and treatment communities, and development of a treatment referral system for the churches.

PNH plans to expand this Project SAVE model to other interfaith groups in the community. The growing trend within communities to participate in the fight against crime and disorder has paralleled a growing recognition by police that traditional crime-fighting tactics alone have limited impact on controlling crime. Community policing is the synthesis of these two movements.

The foundations of successful community policing strategy are the close mutually beneficial ties between police and community members, community partnership and problem solving. Thus, community policing consists of two complementary core components: community partnership and problem solving. The goal of community policing is to reduce crime and disorder by carefully examining the characteristics of problems in neighborhoods, and then applying appropriate problem solving remedies (U.S. Dept. of Justice, 1994).

Community Mobilization

PNH began in March of 1992. A grassroots team had already assembled people active in the community even before the official start of Project Neighborhood. Almost immediately, PNH began to create inroads in the community's struggle to address the toll Alcohol, Tobacco, and Other Drugs were exacting from the neighborhoods.

Built upon the premise that the community is the best possible source for defining community problems and implementing solutions, PNH solicits input from a broad spectrum of residents. Programs are developed to meet the specifications and needs as defined by the community. All programs are planned proactively from an outcome based perspective. Three major accomplishments of PNH mobilizers are noted: (1) greater community involvement and ownership of community problems and solutions, (2) risk factor reduction in the target environment, and (3) linkages of resources to the needs of the community (see Appendices D, E, and F).

Community Policing

In 1993, PNH brought the concept of community policing to Kansas. The Executive Director of PNH, Keith Brown, introduced the idea of community policing to the KCPD Chief Bishop, Mayor Emmanuel Cleaver, Prosecutor Claire McCaskill, and a host of other community leaders. Community policing is, in essence, a collaboration between the police and the community that identifies and solves community problems. Today, PNH works closely with law enforcement officials as they strive to keep the "community" in community policing. A recent KCPD report reveals that in some areas where community policing has been instituted, the crime rate has dropped by 60 percent. An overall decline of the crime rate in Kansas City has been reported to be in the range of 15 to 20 percent.

In conclusion, it is important to note that an analysis of a recent (*Kansas City Star,* May 19, 1996) FBI crime statistics report shows a significant new trend in Kansas City. According to the report, Kansas City's overall crime and homicide rates have dropped from the top ten among the largest U.S. cities. The report shows the homicide rate falling from 9th in the nation in 1994 to 16th in 1995.

In the broad measure of overall crime, which also includes property crimes, Kansas City dropped from fifth in 1994 to 11th. However, Kansas City did remain in the top ten for its violent-crime rate which includes murders, rapes, robberies and assaults. The city dropped only one place, from eighth to ninth, in the rankings. The city's 24 percent drop in its murder rate from 1994 tripled the national 8 percent decline. "From a statistical point of view things look very favorable here and it's good news," said Police Chief Floyd Bartch. "It's hard to identify exactly what has happened." But the city can take some credit in that they have embraced community policing. If this assessment is correct, PNH has much to celebrate because, after all, community policing in

Kansas City was the brain child of PNH. But, as they say in Africa, "it takes a whole village to raise a child."

8

Community Exchange: An Imperative in Substance Abuse Policy Development

Tamara J. Cadet, MPH

What is a Community Exchange?

Communities across America are working to develop community-wide comprehensive strategies and new alliances to address the range of problems associated with the unlawful use of alcohol and drugs. There have been many successes, and the leaders have gained expertise that is unique, rich, and as varied as the communities in which they work. It is this valuable knowledge and experience, shared by community leaders, that can be made available to America's cities, towns, and neighborhoods in an innovative, peer to peer technical assistance model—The Community Exchange. Community Exchange is a product of Join Together, a National Resource for communities fighting substance abuse. It is funded by the Robert Wood Johnson Foundation through the Boston University School of Public Health. Community exchange is a tool with a strategic planning process that a community can use to move their substance abuse agenda forward. Some communities use it to involve more people in the issues, others choose to impact public policy.

In April 1991, the Robert Wood Johnson Foundation made a planning grant to review the state of support programs for community coalitions to address substance abuse. The central question posed in that proposal was "whether these thousand flowers will bloom into a beautiful cross-pollinated perennial garden or whether they will shine briefly and wither in isolation." Join Together's goals were developed from the examination of the following areas:

- The experience of Fighting Back to date;
- The experience and plans for the then Office for Substance Abuse Prevention Partnership Program, including its training and technical assistance efforts;
- The experience and plans for the President's Advisory Committee Drug Abuse Coalition Taskforce;
- The experience and plans of other federal government agencies supporting community coalitions;
- The needs and desires of a number of community coalition leaders for additional support, particularly their views on how to get new information, how they relate to their colleagues, and the kinds of policy barriers they encounter;
- The experience of other foundations in supporting community-based programs in health and other fields;
- The experience and views of state level substance officials;
- The views of evaluators and social scientists who have studied community-based activities and substance abuse programs;
- The options for developing electronic networks for people in this field, and the experience of people in similar fields in developing and using such tools.

These aforementioned reviews answer the questions about "who is doing what," and the gaps that exist in training, technical assistance, diffusion, and policy development. Some of the themes that emerged from the reviews include: (1) Community coalition as a term means different things to different people. It may mean grassroots movement through which people are empowered to defeat substance abuse in their community, or it may mean that people with power—the government, business and professional leaders—use their power to defeat it; (2) Community coalitions are central in working against substance abuse, but are vulnerable to failure. Some of the issues identified relate to the skills and long-term commitment of the people leading the work, an inability to break through institutional barriers and policies that impede the work and a failure in existing government programs to foster broad cooperation among different actors and agencies. In "Fighting Drug Abuse at the Local Level," by Paul S. Jellinek and Ruby P. Hearn, it is noted that local efforts, together with national programs such as the intensive media campaign being conducted by the Partnership for a Drug-Free America, are beginning to make a difference. However, the demand side has not

An Imperative in Substance Abuse Policy Development 125

been given a fair test. Despite the proliferation of local demand-reduction programs and activities, there has been little attempt to tie such endeavors together. Overall, projects have spontaneously started. There is no common understanding of the problem, no consensus regarding priorities, and as a result, no overall strategy for deploying a community's multiple resources in a focused, unified effort. One of the original goals for Join Together: A National Resource for Communities Fighting Substance Abuse was to speed the diffusion of innovative and effective programs to communities. The objective to meet this goal was to establish community site visits and a technical assistance model to foster this diffusion to reduce substance abuse. A hypothesis that formed the basis of the goal was the following:

> Communities which have frequent involvement with Join Together, by participation in site visits, computer network, and training programs will show more progress in reducing the harms from substance abuse as measured by indicators developed by Join Together, than communities without these experiences.

Community exchange is highlighted by a two-day event with a team of visiting community leaders. These leaders share their ideas, strategies on success, obstacles, and challenges on what has and has not worked for their particular communities. This team, Community Exchange Visitors, shares their strategies and ideas in a variety of ways. Visitors can be a part of business and legislative breakfasts, or specialized meetings designed to get clergy members more involved. Press conferences and editorial meetings may be part of the two days as well as youth speak-outs. The community knows and determines what events will draw the entire community. The design of the two days are (1) to get community motivated to do something about an issue; (2) create more awareness about the work being done, and (3) to celebrate successes or a new alliance that has been made to further the substance abuse agenda of a community. Most importantly, the ways in which the team share their information is designed by the community to meet the needs of the community. It is truly up to the community how those days are designed.

Framingham, Massachusetts, provides a good example of a community exchange. The theme was "Youth and Business as Resources in Creating a Healthier Framingham Community." This community group wanted to bring youth and business persons together to do something. The youth had complained that business did not care about them, and did not give them jobs. The business community, on the other hand, said that youth did not need jobs. The business community never even thought of youth as a possible partner or resource to work together. The visiting community leaders from Miami (Florida), Syracuse (New York), and Bridgeport (Connecticut) were matched with the Framingham groups based on their expertise and experience working in this area. The visitor from Miami worked with youth and developed a youth leadership program. He was able to share with the youth about how to develop their leadership so they appealed to the business owners. He shared strategies about how the youth from Miami have worked successfully with the business community. From Syracuse, the visitor shared her coalition's strategies on how partnerships between any two groups in a community can work. The visitor from Bridgeport shared how his business got involved with coalition activities, and the role his business plays with youth. Today, as a result of the community exchange, a Business/Youth Task Force has been established as part of the Framingham community and is operating in its fourth year. In addition, businesses are now providing jobs and scholarships to the youth that work for them.

Goals and Objectives

It is the aim of the community exchange to accomplish the following goals:

- Increase in networking,
- Work on common substance abuse problems,
- Refocus community strategic plan,
- Gain media exposure, and
- Increase in resources/funding.

Each community that Join Together has worked with on this model has had varying degrees of meeting these goals. Goals must be based on what outcomes the community wanted to achieve. For example, Tallahassee, Florida, received an Area Health Education Center grant to begin a church-based health program after working with a minister from Mobile, Alabama. Oswego, New York, had an eight-page pullout in their local paper covering the newly-formed coalition and the community exchange they hosted. In San Luis Obispo, California, over 150 community leaders are now participating in developing a community-wide substance abuse strategic plan whereas before the community exchange there had been only a few. It must be clear that it is important for the community to establish its goals, as any organization would do when beginning a strategic planning process.

Community exchange is based on research which suggests that a "practitioner-based" approach to technical assistance is more effective than a "professional-consultant" approach. Join Together conducted a series of focus groups in 1994 throughout the country and found that "community [groups] are in need of technical assistance that is provided by peer practitioners who are actively working in [their] communities as opposed to an 'expert-consultant' model" (Join Together, 1994).

Community exchange represents Join Together's philosophy that reductions in substance abuse can be best achieved by creating comprehensive, community-wide strategies encompassing all sectors of the community and problems. They include: public awareness, prevention, early identification, treatment, aftercare, job training, law enforcement, illicit drugs, alcohol regulation, underage drinking, tobacco control, funding for substance abuse services, community development, public policy, sustaining coalitions, and recruiting new leadership. A strategy usually includes:

- *Specific goals.* For example, "the percentage of kids who try to use marijuana should go down every year."
- *Programs and policies that are related to achieving established goals.* For example, student and parent marijuana prevention education, anti-marijuana media spots, youth-run activities, targeted action against sellers of paraphernalia and cigarette paper, etc.
- *Ways to monitor progress toward the goals.* For example, regular school surveys that measure use of marijuana by young people in communities.
- *A regular report of the progress being made and a description of the process for reviewing current goals, programs, and for adjusting them to changing circumstances.* For example, an annual public hearing by the city council to review the community strategy and discuss the progress report (Leading from the Ground Up, The Join Together Third National Survey, p. 26).

In fact, those community groups who responded to the Third National Survey suggest that community groups tend to have more of an impact on substance abuse in their communities when they have a comprehensive strategy than those that do not. An example of what can happen when a community has and uses a strategy is the Tahoe Prevention Network, Lake Tahoe, California. Their written strategy is about identifying risk factors and developing ways to overcome them. They came to this conclusion based on a community needs assessment conducted. The assessment identified four areas the Tahoe Prevention Network focuses on: *community, schools, family, and individuals/peers*. For each of these areas, the Tahoe Prevention Network developed projects that built resiliency to lower the risks of substance abuse. One risk factor in the schools is the high student turnover level due to the transient nature of this area. Tahoe Prevention Network dealt with this risk factor by creating a welcome center to help new students quickly adjust to school and to require parents to meet with social service providers as part of the enrollment process.

A comprehensive strategy helps a community working on a community exchange to be more successful because the community understands and knows what its goals are and how to accomplish them. A community needs to be as clear as possible about its goals so they know what type of experiences and expertise they are look for in the community exchange team. The team can be selected based on the goals and issues of the community.

Impact of a Community Exchange

To date, twenty-nine communities have participated in this peer to peer exchange. Each one has been uniquely different because of the different issues/needs defined by the community. The issues are many and varied. They include parent denial and involvement, underage drinking, gang violence, business involvement, youth involvement, and impacting policies. Each one has been uniquely successful, not only to Join Together, but more importantly to the community itself. As part of an impact evaluation conducted by Sanford L. Weiner, Massachusetts Institute of Technology, these key findings were established about the community exchange model:

- The Community Exchange Team is highly valued for its expertise.

- There is great enthusiasm for peer consultants.
- The high quality, high visibility events lead to increased local participation and commitment.
- Over time, increased participation leads to multiple positive outcomes for the community.

If we go back to the original goals of the community exchange and take a look at the following examples, one can see the potential impact the community exchange has on a given community.

- *Increase in Networking.* Amherst, New York, tripled coalition membership, including faith, business, and criminal justice communities; launched a new local policy initiative; and linked itself with a nearby urban community to work on common problems.
- *Work on Common Problems.* Kankakee, Illinois, has for the first time involvement of the inter-faith community, resulting in a task force. Kankakee also strengthened the linkages between the criminal justice system and the community task force, resulting in the formation of a drug court.
- *Refocus Strategic Plan.* Arecibo, Puerto Rico, expanded a community partnership into three other communities, formed a viable coalition with business leaders, established new alliances that led to three new federal grants, and began a regional collaborative strategic plan.
- *Media Exposure to Issues.* Belleville, New Jersey, revitalized a five-year-old successful business coalition, established a new local ordinance, raised community awareness, and has formed an alliance with the local newspaper which now runs weekly columns on the coalition's activities.
- *Increase in Resources/Funding.* Tallahassee, Florida, not only received funding to begin the church-based health program, but the youth committee of the coalition became an official 4-H Club, resulting in a permanent organizational and institutional home as well as receiving leadership development opportunities.

Community exchange has had an impact on those communities that have participated, and have concrete outcomes to show for their work. These community groups also had comprehensive strategies which allowed for so many successes. As mentioned earlier, those community groups with written comprehensive strategies tend to be more successful in having an impact on substance abuse than those without. This finding also relates to the community exchange model in that the best organized local groups were able to make more of the specific events during the two days. They were also more successful in terms of public awareness and turnout. In addition, they were more ready with follow-up work, including establishing programs and committees that need to occur to take advantage of the momentum generated by the community exchange.

It should be clear at this point that a community exchange is and can be a vehicle to move a community from one level of work to another level. A community exchange can assist in mobilizing community members to action. It is nothing more than a tool—a tool that can be part of any community's strategy to reduce the harms of substance abuse. It is a tool to advance public policy work.

Public Policy and Communities

Changes in public policy can have a major effect on how successful a community is in preventing and reducing substance abuse. It is no longer confined to city hall or the state legislature. Public policy is more than changing laws. It is more than the legislation and ordinances that federal and state officials set. Public policy includes changing norms and practices, which should happen at the local level. Public policy change is prevention. It is intervention. It is treatment. It is aftercare. It is law enforcement. It is economic development. Public policy can regulate the [substance abuse] environment in a community. It is important for [communities] to understand how to use public policy for changes. Anything that affects the health, safety, and well-being of the public and individual involves public policy (Join Together, "Strategies," Summer 1994, insert). Therefore, public policy change encompasses all of substance abuse and it needs to be a priority in the substance abuse field. Work cannot be done on underage drinking without looking at community norms, community practices, prevention programs, treatment programs, and law enforcement programs as well as local ordinances, regulations, and laws.

Join Together has convened several National Public Policy Panels on various substance abuse topics. One reason was because community leaders said that public policy was one of their principal barriers to success. Communities need to address public policy issues in order to meet their goals. Public policy had been identified as a major barrier in the Join Together 1992 survey. While that may have been true, only 57 percent

An Imperative in Substance Abuse Policy Development 131

of community groups (total N = 1910) responding to the 1995 Third National Survey are likely to be involved in efforts to change public policy. In fact, public policy work is important, however, it is not a major priority for a coalition or community.

When asked if there had been public policy changes in communities where coalitions existed, the following was reported in the 1995 Join Together National Survey, "Leading from the Ground Up—The Third Survey of the Community Movement Against Substance Abuse":

- More than half reported that there have been changes in drinking and driving laws and tobacco regulations in the past two years.
- 33 percent reported changes in alcohol regulation.
- 25 percent reported tobacco tax increases.
- 14 percent reported alcohol tax increases.

It is obvious some public policy changes are occurring. However, when asked if coalitions had been involved in these changes, they reported:

- Fewer than half of the coalitions were involved in passing any of the public policy changes that were reported.
- An average of 44 percent say they were involved in tobacco, alcohol, and drunk driving changes.
- Only one-quarter had been involved in implementing tax increases (D. Rosenbloom, Third National Survey, p. 21).

These numbers again make it clear that public policy change is not a priority for communities, and needs to be in order to make a substantial impact on substance abuse in this country.

It is very interesting that while community groups may not be as much involved as they need to be, community leaders do have views of policies they need to be more effective. They believe in a broad-based approach—a systemic-wide change is needed. Focusing on one piece of substance abuse will just not work. Focusing on prevention without law enforcement, treatment, and others will not work. Community leaders want prevention work supported by public policies that send strong and consistent messages against illicit drugs and excessive alcohol use.

- 98 percent favor additional restrictions on alcohol and tobacco advertising.

- 95 percent want increased taxes on alcohol because higher prices will reduce use by young people.
- 80 percent support random drug testing in the workplace since the majority of drug users are employed.
- 70 percent even support similar testing in the schools to send messages—messages that drug use and drinking at work or school is unacceptable.

Regarding *law enforcement policies*:

- 95 percent of community leaders support increased local police enforcement of drug, alcohol, and tobacco laws.
- 79 percent oppose decriminalizing possession.
- 87 percent oppose decriminalizing sales of currently illicit drugs.
- 82 percent favor increased penalties for sales of illicit drugs.
- 73 percent want stronger penalties for possession.

Policies to support treatment from community leaders show that:

- 55 percent of leaders strongly support that "treatment be available for everyone who needs it, immediately."
- 94 percent believe that treatment should be mandatory for non-violent offenders who have drug or alcohol problems.
- 68 percent favor "needle exchange" programs to prevent the spread of HIV.

Some of this is about changing laws, but it is also about changing the way a community does business as it relates to substance abuse. When a community decides to change norms, then law-changing can follow. But the community must be motivated enough or understand that norms need to change. Then, they have begun to tackle public policy. Public policy issues may vary, but they can all be linked to substance abuse. These numbers are the same or have increased since the 1992 and 1993 Join Together National Surveys were released. Notice that law enforcement and treatment are listed as policies. If a community decides to conduct random drug testing in the schools, it should be assumed that prevention people, treatment people, education people, parents, and youth have begun to work together to accomplish the reduction of drug use among youth. The community has changed a practice. It has started to implement a policy that is outcome-based.

Public policy changes do occur in communities. There will be fewer liquor stores built in South Central Los Angeles, thanks to that community's strong position on limiting the number of outlets there. Baltimore, Maryland, tackled tobacco and alcohol billboard advertising in 1994 and were able to ban billboards from residential areas. Health care reform was the public policy issue for communities in Columbus, Ohio, and Los Alamos, New Mexico, where town meetings educated people about the importance of including substance abuse benefits.

How Can Community Exchange Be a Tool in Public Policy

A community exchange is a tool to assist communities in changing community norms and practices, and essentially public policy. It is a tool that can help communities change regulations, ordinances, and laws. As mentioned earlier, a community exchange gives a community an opportunity to come together and strategize about a particular issue. No matter what that issue is, public policy is going to play a role, and a community should consider this if residents are planning to use the community exchange model.

As mentioned earlier, in 1992 Join Together began to convene National Public Policy Panels as a way to reduce the policy barriers faced by communities. Policy panels are only one element of a strong policy program, which also includes advocacy efforts for local, state, and federal officials. However, the panels are also a tool that can be all of, part of, or follow-up to a community exchange. A panel can be looked at as a public forum. Many communities have held town meetings such as Columbus, Ohio, and Los Alamos, New Mexico, as part of their community exchange. Panels are a useful way for generating public awareness of substance abuse issues within a given community. They serve as a means of promoting coordinated, strategic planning and specific initiatives that support the strategic goals. In addition, panels are useful networking tools.

Prevention advocates in San Diego County convened a local policy panel on youth access to alcohol. While it may not have gone under the guise of community exchange, the panel proved to be a powerful organizing tool for focusing public attention to the problems of underage drinking and youth access to alcohol. The local panel provided community members with an organizing framework and a coordinated plan for local efforts as well as for involving new people. To date, a number of initiatives have emerged. Some include: media campaigns at two local high schools on zero tolerance youth driving laws; local school districts and DARE coordinators have received training about policy options; and the city of San Diego has formed a task force to evaluate how to use liquor laws to develop strong accountability on alcohol laws. These are initiatives that may not have occurred without the panel. As one can see, the outcomes of a policy panel as a tool alone or particularly as part of the community exchange can meet the goals of increasing networking capability; working on common substance abuse problems; refocusing a community strategic plan; working with media; and increasing resources/funding.

When working with communities, Join Together asks a series of questions to assist communities in developing their strategies. The questions include:

- What is the policy you are addressing?
- How do you know it is a problem? What harm is it causing or what good is it preventing?
- What specific change would you find ideal? How do you know it will be better?
- Where is the policy "located"? What is its origin? Who are its current beneficiaries and supporters? How do you know that?
- Who would be your allies in making a change? How can you get additional people to develop a mutual interest?
- What kind of issue or event can you use to demonstrate the need and benefit for change? How can communities raise the visibility of the issue?
- What are the alternative ways to get what you want? Is there some step that will get you most of what you need?
- If you get to change the policy, what must you do in order to take full advantage?
- What must you do to make sure that any victory on this issue strengthens you for future efforts on the other issues? Conversely, what must you do to insure that victory, loss, or delay does not weaken you for future efforts?

Community exchanges mobilize community residents to action. Notice the impacts mentioned with several community exchange descriptions. They all had a policy link to them. In Kansas City, Missouri, their community exchange focused on two broad policy issues: youth and environment. Project Neighborhood, Inc., found that in order to begin to address underage access to alcohol and drugs, absentee landlordism, violence, and alternative places for youth to play, they first had to deal with the public policies supporting or not supporting these aforementioned issues. The residents of Kansas City want underage drinking and drug use to stop, but store owners are selling to minors. Drug dealing is evident on the streets. Youth do not have an alternative place to hang out. Look at the existing policies. How can the residents of Kansas City have policies enforced so that minors are not being sold alcoholic beverages? They need to work with the store owners and law enforcement. The community exchange will give each group a forum to express their ideas and frustrations facilitated by a community exchange visitor from Detroit, Michigan, who has been very successful in changing underage access to alcohol policies in her community. Another community exchange visitor from Jamaica Plain, Massachusetts, problem-solved issues of underage access to drugs. It is connected to the fact that youth do not have a place to hang out. Perhaps the Kansas City community will look at using public school buildings or other facilities as recreational centers. In order to accomplish this, they must look at what policies are existing. Do they need to be amended or changed, and who can they build an alliance with to achieve this goal? Again, the community exchange is a viable medium to make this dialogue occur. So often in communities, mobilization and action just need a forum for dialogue and a community exchange can be that tool.

Absentee landlordism is a concern among residents in Kansas City. They want their community to be safe and clean. When landlords buy property in a neighborhood but do not invest in the neighborhood's well-being, houses become run down and may even become drug dealing dens. Kansas City residents do not want this occurring in their neighborhoods. They are using the community exchange as a viable opportunity to bring landlords, residents, housing developers, and other interested parties together on a panel to discuss strategies and solutions. This panel was facilitated by a community leader from Baltimore, Maryland, who has been very successful in working with absentee landlords as well as with communities dealing with vacant houses.

All the issues deal with substance abuse whether it is stated in name or not. This connection of substance abuse and other social issues, crime, violence, and health care is clear at the community level. It is not always so clear at the state and federal levels. As mentioned earlier when talking about policy panels, part of public policy work for local groups includes advocacy to help clearly establish these links for the state and federal policymakers. This can begin to happen at the community exchange. It can be part of the follow-up work. It is part of creating a system change.

How Can Community Exchange Be a Tool to Prevention Resource Systems

Public policy is part of a comprehensive, community-wide strategic plan. A community cannot begin to think about impacting the way substance abuse affects them without including public policy change in that plan. Remember, comprehensive strategies address all areas of substance abuse. In a Prevention Resource System, a broad-based approach—a systemic wide change is imperative. A community is looking at strategies to promote the health of itself—a healthy community. To have healthy communities, every individual, community group, agency, and organization must be at the table. Everyone has a stake in a healthy community. This is what a prevention resource system is about. With a system in place, the harms from substance abuse can be prevented and reduced. The community exchange is a model, a mechanism, a tool to encourage the dialogue to motivate people to join together to make public policy change. Communities can plan a community exchange without the direct assistance of Join Together to create a prevention resource system. In Columbus, Ohio, they are currently planning a Franklin County Community Exchange using their community resources. Their goals are the same as the Join Together model.

Local communities can make policies a part of the system, a part of the prevention resource system. Institutionalize them! In thinking about community exchange and the prevention resource system, remember the following:

- Know what you are trying to accomplish;
- Listen to the problems as they are experienced by the people;
- Know what outcomes you want to achieve; and most of all,
- Hold the belief that the community has the answer!

An Imperative in Substance Abuse Policy Development 137

If efforts to reduce substance abuse in America's cities, communities, and neighborhoods are to be successful, effective approaches to mobilize the community to make public policy choices are imperative. The community exchange approach is a proven successful model.

9

Recommendations

This chapter summarizes the recommendations made by the four workshops at the symposium.

These workshops focused on key structural components of prevention resource systems: (1) prevention infrastructure, (2) prevention networks, (3) systemic support, and (4) research and evaluation. Two academics, Professor Edith Freeman of the University of Kansas and Dr. Mary Jo Larson of Brandeis University provided the summaries on Prevention Networks and Research and Evaluation, respectively. Janine Lee, a foundation senior officer, developed the systematic support paper. James Copple, a national expert on coalition building, guided the report on Prevention Infrastructure.

The following are specific recommendations by the workshops.

Group A: Prevention Infrastructure
by James Copple

RECOMMENDATION 1. Project Neighborhood Youth Task Force

Project Neighborhood will establish a youth task force to implement specific youth focused policies, practices, and procedures related to the mission of Project Neighborhood. The task force will meet monthly, be broad-based and established on high school geographic boundaries, and will be diverse in ethnicity, race, geography, and gender. Their activities will include, but will not be limited to the following: (a) Publication of a newsletter, (b) Create and maintain television and radio programs on public access channels, (c) Work to create counter-advertising

140 Recommendations

campaigns, (d) Monitor all alcohol and drug related violence programs to assure youth participation on governing boards and policy panels, (e) Work with community-based organizations and law enforcement to discuss youth security patrols.

RECOMMENDATION 2. **Mayor's Youth Task Force**
This task force should meet with the Mayor and the City Council to carry out community initiatives as mutually determined by city officials and members of Project Neighborhood. The Mayor's Task Force would be responsible for implementing specific programs aimed at Kansas City youth.

RECOMMENDATION 3. **Superintendent's Youth Task Force**
This task force should meet with the Superintendent or Board of Education to carry out school-based initiatives mutually determined by the Superintendent and members of Project Neighborhood. The Superintendent's Task Force would be responsible for implementing specific programs aimed at schools and school community initiatives.

RECOMMENDATION 4. **Police Youth Task Force**
This task force should meet with the Chief of Police or Police Advisory Council to carry out community policing initiatives mutually determined by the Chief of Police and members of Project Neighborhood. The Police Youth Task Force would be responsible for implementing specific programs aimed at improving police and youth understanding and collaboration on programs designed to improve safety.

RECOMMENDATION 5. **Chamber of Commerce Youth Task Force**
This task force should meet with the President and Executive Director of the Kansas City Chamber of Commerce to carry out business and enterprise activities aimed at youth employment. The Chamber of Commerce Youth Task Force would be responsible for implementing specific programs aimed at improving communications between Kansas City youth and the business community. This is a vehicle for school-to-work programs.

Strategies
These strategies reflect ideas about the Kansas City the participants wanted to create.

WHEN WE ARE FINISHED—WHERE DO WE WANT TO BE?
1. Economic and social stability in our communities
2. Increased communications among all sectors of the community
3. Adults listen to youth in all Project Neighborhood Forums
4. Empowerment Zone resources targeted to specific neighborhoods
5. Examined the problems with forced integration in schooling, policing and other areas of community development
6. Make educational institutions more responsive to youth and to neighborhoods
7. Provide parenting skills so parents can more accurately communicate with their children
8. Systematically examine alternatives to incarceration
9. Identify organizations that are prepared to recognize and affirm the accomplishments of youth
10. Build programs that integrate youth with the elder population

Group B: Prevention Networks
by Edith M. Freeman

RECOMMENDATION:
1. The youth recommend that existing prevention networks, future symposia, and any follow-up activities to the current symposium shift from formal presentations and speakers to a more informal youth-oriented format: experiential activities, games, and participatory tasks or exercises.
2. Recovering people in the community should develop a prevention advocacy network similar to those developed by groups with other chronic and genetic-based diseases in order to lobby for more funding for addiction and prevention research, programming, and better enforcement of existing substance abuse laws.
3. Youth should develop peer networks that help prevent addiction or that reach out to youth currently using drugs and alcohol. The network is needed as a form of personal accountability among youth.
4. Many of the existing prevention networks need to come together to do joint planning in the following areas since none of them are currently addressing these areas:
   - How to reach youth already in trouble with drugs and alcohol (they are isolated, fearful, ashamed, and have low self-esteem).

142 Recommendations

- How to reduce competition between the networks for funding and serve certain groups of children and youth/special programming areas.
- Reducing the accessibility of drugs and alcohol to youth.
- Better enforcement of existing laws designed for prevention.
- The development of a more effective overall, organized, and systematic approach to prevention (compared to current traditional approaches that do not work, especially with youth).

5. Involve youth more fully in prevention through service on agency Boards of Directors and in prevention network committees and other activities.
6. Prevention networks should use their influence to make prevention programs more effective through the following:
   - Give peers an active role in prevention services to other youth.
   - Use more youth-oriented activities as prevention strategies compared to the current method of "talking at" youth.
   - Sponsor more long term prevention efforts rather than one-shot approaches that do not include follow-up. If short-term prevention approaches are used, then some type of ongoing follow-up is needed in order for prevention with youth to be effective.
   - Include aspects of faith and spirituality in prevention, using games and mentors to focus the education/information at the youths' level.
   - Include cultural, ethnic, and gender education in all prevention programs and strategies.
   - Focus more funding and emphasis on prevention with young children than the current effort.
   - Include special drug and alcohol education for drug dealers as part of prevention.
   - Create youth incentives as part of prevention programs: access to jobs, job training, career information, and other strategies.

Group C: Systemic Support for Prevention
by Janine Lee

RECOMMENDATION: Informing the Government

1. Communities organize to put pressure on the political leadership to invest money (from the 1/4 cent sales tax) into *prevention vs.* enforcement.

2. More community involvement (neighborhood and grassroots) in decision-making regarding allocation of dollars.

RECOMMENDATION: Developing a Plan

Neighbors, parents, youth and other community leaders come together to develop a prevention funding and resource plan. This would represent a "community" planning table that Team C does not feel currently exists in Kansas City.

RECOMMENDATION: Family/Community Support

Involvement of parents, family and community to get their commitment to prevention; and educate them regarding the consequences of substance abuse.

Youth:
- Develop co-op youth boards.
- Youth group discussions involving all aspects of the community.

Church:
- Increased church involvement with substance abuse issues.

Communications:
- Communicate to our community how important prevention is, collaboration among organizations, providers.
- National model for quarter-cent sales tax.
- Youth request: Community centers have internet access "on-line." This communication opens our community to global knowledge and resources.

Evaluation:
- Make sure that programs are evaluated in quality, not just quantity.

Funding Strategies:
- Lottery, raffles, grants, investments.
- Foundations, youth enterprise, national donation
- Recover agency for prevention

Group D: Prevention Research & Evaluation
by Mary Jo Larson

KEY RECOMMENDATION 1: Youth consumers and their parents should be our KEY informants on how well the prevention network is performing. This will require a revolution in the way we conduct assessments because few mechanisms currently tap into youth opinions.

Action Steps:
1. Seven youth volunteered to join the existing Project Neighborhood Prevention Committee. Phone numbers were exchanged and there was conversation about transportation needs, etc.
2. To avoid burn out of a few key young people, several youth volunteered to recruit or identify other young people who could participate in discussion groups with providers interested in evaluating their services.
3. Several providers committed themselves to forming "key informant" panels of young people. This would be one way to solicit first hand feed back on how well their programs were doing.
4. Youth suggested that the prevention network sponsor events to pull a broad group of young people together. The type of event that would be popular would be a dance. This would be a time to gather information and opinions from a broader group of people.

KEY RECOMMENDATION 2: Young people should help us gather field data in our studies. They should be a part of our research teams, bringing in information that might otherwise be inaccessible to us.

Action Steps:
1. The prevention network should offer training to youth on a variety of topics to prepare them to participate on our committees and in our field research. This investment could include skill-building in group facilitation; interviewing techniques; how to record observations.
2. The prevention network could invest in a camcorder that would be used by investigative teams of youth who are willing to interview people in the neighborhood and on street corners.

KEY RECOMMENDATION 3: We should share our research findings with the top layers of the city in order to attract additional resources for the prevention network. We want some of our research to affect their resources, actions, and decisions. We also want to hold the prevention network accountable for accomplishing results. This will help attract additional resources.

Action Steps:
1. To participate in existing review and strategy-setting mechanisms within the community. For example, the Kaufmann Foundation has a Youth Committee that helps inform them of local needs and assessments. The Vision 2000 is planning a meeting in December that will focus on Citywide Health Promotion.
2. We should develop new mechanisms to disseminate credible, reliable information as well. One such mechanism might be a "preventive report card" that monitors whether or not the prevention network is performing as it is intended (see more discussion below).

KEY RECOMMENDATION 4: The prevention network should share success stories among all prevention providers and more broadly as well. There is a need to celebrate our success not in a competitive way, but in a way that demonstrates that prevention works and to help all programs improve. While the immediate audience may be prevention providers or the COMBAT providers, we should share with parents, schools, and the broader community too.

Action Steps:
1. Use the existing newsletters in neighborhoods, among COMBAT providers, through the community extension service.
2. Explore novel ideas, such as replace the unwanted billboard messages in local neighborhoods with new messages about our successes.
3. Tie into the youth radio station, "KC Teen Shows", and let youth determine the format for spreading the prevention success stories.

KEY RECOMMENDATION 5: We should honor and exalt the positive change that individuals make, and recognize them for their personal success.

10

Where Do We Go From Here?

Jacob U. Gordon, Ph.D.

In one of his books, *Where Do We Go From Here?* (King Jr., 1968), the late civil rights leader, Dr. Martin Luther King, Jr., urged his fellow citizens in America not to choose chaos but civil communities. The communities Dr. King Jr. envisioned were to be free of racism, communities where there was to be respect for human dignity, free of substance abuse and violence, communities that care, and above all communities where all God's children can work together to improve human sufferings and their quality of life. This volume has attempted to demonstrate that where we must go from here requires systems change, a change from investing in what does not work to more investment in what we know already works. We know that prisons don't work, so why invest and expand the prison industry? On the other hand, there is ample evidence that the Head Start program works, so why not invest more in Head Start for America's future? Similarly, while national policies and practices against alcohol, tobacco and other drugs have not produced any expected outcome and impact, the Robert Wood Johnson Foundation's Fighting Back national demonstration project, designed to reduce alcohol and other drug abuse, is working in several communities. Its ability to impact systems change in Kansas City, Missouri should not only be applauded but replicated throughout America's inner cities. Major features for a systems change model in substance abuse area should be noted.

Guiding Principles for Prevention Resource Systems

Because prevention resource systems are complex, dynamic and involve a potentially ever-increasing number of participants, they must rely on a clear set of integrated guiding principles.

The following list of guiding principles is a foundation for development, and will no doubt grow as prevention resource systems discover additional principles.

Be diverse, inclusive and politically bipartisan. To be fully accountable and successful, diversity should cross lines of culture, gender, orientation, ethnicity, role race and ableness, as well as politics, mandates and funding categories. Single agendas cannot dominate. All participants, and their cultural perspectives, are viewed as potential resources for problem solving.

Be public. Being public requires people to listen carefully to many voices. It requires people to listen carefully to the norms that shape others' experiences, interests and world views. The prevention resource system is accessible to all citizens. Differences and personal biases have to be put aside long enough to listen effectively and work collectively.

Be advocates. Members of prevention resource systems are committed to sustain, support, subsidize and serve as a "voice" for prevention work. The prevention resource system serves as the "head and heart" for its individual and collective prevention work, providing the fundamental principles, practices and core support for effective programs and services.

Establish, maintain and support integrated delivery systems. Technical assistance is available for all components. Multiple approaches are available as are multiple strategies. The delivery systems are need and outcome driven, and change as needs and desired outcomes emerge. The expectation is that providers of programs and services are involved in ongoing skill and leadership development. Training and learning experiences are strategic in nature and key organizing tools. The system is supported by traditional funding and resources.

Be pragmatic, visionary and anchored by problems to be solved and new realities to create. The primary purpose of prevention resource systems is to be pragmatic visionaries; to solve public problems and to create new realities that support safety, health and opportunity. Lacking a concern, need or shared vision, the prevention resource, as defined here, would not exist. Assessing public needs and a shared vision for the future is an ongoing process, which must integrate changing concerns and emerging issues. The prevention resource system is proactive, dynamic and evolving. Participants in the prevention resource system hold problems in common—such as education, health, crime—but they frequently have diverse interests in relation to the problem, which must be taken into account. Solutions and strategies are developed based on current and evolving research and conceptual frameworks, using multiple delivery systems.

Be characterized by dialog, debate, argument and conflict. People often do not agree. Interests conflict. Yet, conflict is needed to develop full solutions that are able to work for more than just one group. Diverse participants can teach each other useful skills and models for effective problem solving and conflict resolution.

Reconceptualize power. In traditional hierarchical structures, power and information often reside at the "top" of the organization. Within prevention resource systems, power resides in all of the components, played out in clear, interdependent roles and responsibilities. Information is open and shared, creating and supporting a learning community that involves all members learning and sharing knowledge on behalf of the system. Leadership opportunities are plentiful. Leadership is shared, distributed and revolving, with emerging leaders identified as they work to develop their capacities for action and problem solving.

Develop accountability through public evaluation. People see the relationship between their knowledge and capacity and the problems to be solved. They assume roles and responsibilities accordingly, build appropriate relationships, share resources, experience the complexities of public decision-making and collaborative action. Evaluation is incorporated throughout the process, in all components. New strategies for evaluation are explored and applied to determine usefulness. Evaluation systems meet accountability needs through assessment of both targeted outcome measures, as well as the working process of the system itself.

Provide regulatory balance. The prevention resource system supports and upholds local, state, and federal regulations, policies, laws, and mandates. In addition, the system is creative in seeking technical assistance, legislation and waivers when regulations prohibit or become barriers to being successful in prevention work. Lastly, the system is a champion of individual constitutional rights.

Model commitment. Participants, as appropriate, commit to the system by establishing multi-agency agreements, pooling resources, and seeking opportunities for collaborative action whenever possible, based upon the mutually determined strategic goals of the system. Levels of participation may change over time, and agreements renegotiated, as appropriate.

Support and model leadership. To create an environment that is supportive of cross agency/interest boundaries, the prevention resource system needs leaders who value the conceptual framework, see its usefulness, and are willing to take risks as they bring the prevention resource system concept to their arenas. Certain leadership capacities are integrally woven into this leadership role and should be cultivated whenever possible. Leadership includes: a valuing of diversity and inclusion, a passion for democratic ideals, and an enjoyment of a political arena; relation give and take, interactive and sometimes messy processes and dimensions of the public arena; an ability to do strategic and systems thinking and "map" desired outcomes; a keen interest in the conceptual framework for prevention resource systems; an ability to model, act, teach, and organize; a willingness to experiment, along with the ability to tolerate ambiguity, uncertainty and chaos; an ability to creatively manage conflict; a willingness to carry new messages; the ability to be self-evaluating and reflective; and a determination to step aside and encourage and mentor emerging leaders.

Core Structural Components of Prevention Resource Systems

In order to develop the concept of Prevention Resource Systems in operational terms, it will be useful for us to look at four interdependent structural components within such a system: the community, prevention infrastructures, prevention networks and systemic support for prevention work.

Communities: The Foundation. We start with communities as the foundation component because all prevention work is ultimately implemented at the local level, in community settings, by individuals working through groups and organizations, over time. It is a complex undertaking, requiring a variety of information skills and resources, combined in focused ways that will achieve specific outcomes and changes.

Experience has shown that community-based prevention work can be dramatically enhanced through the coordinated support of three other prevention resource system components, namely prevention infrastructures, prevention networks, and systematic support.

Prevention Infrastructure: Integrating Policy, Standards, and Resources. A Prevention Infrastructure is made up of all the governmental systems that have a legal mandate to provide prevention leadership, policies and service resources. Based on this working definition, we can see that there are prevention infrastructures that operate at the community level, at the state level and at the federal level. By intentionally operating within a prevention resource system framework, these governmental entities can maximize the effectiveness of government resources and significantly increase the quality of community-based prevention work.

Prevention Networks: Linking Skill with People. A prevention network is a conscious and intentional relationship among prevention service providers who nurture and support communities in their collaborative prevention work. Prevention networks are often the bridge between prevention infrastructures and community-based prevention work.

Prevention networks fueled by resources from prevention infrastructures, provide a wide range of accessible prevention services from direct prevention programming to ongoing training and technical assistance. Prevention networks translate and transform the prevention infrastructure mandates into increased community capacity to do prevention work.

Systemic Support. Experience has shown that social problems are intertwined; they do not exist in net, closed systems. Alcohol abuse is not just about alcohol; in some cases, it's also about teenage pregnancy or domestic violence. Drug abuse is not just about drugs; it's also often crime, poverty, and community conditions that place people at risk.

Prevention successes are strongly linked to interventions that involve participation and resources from many sectors and levels, in ongoing collaborative relationships; a prevention resource system.

Indeed, systems are animated by concerns forged out of people's everyday personal experiences and need. In focusing on intentionally building and maintaining prevention resource systems, we are able to broaden the opportunities for meaningful participation in prevention work, as well as to integrate resources in ways that bring about increased synergism.

Operational Functions with Prevention Resource Systems

Experience has identified fifteen core operating functions within prevention resource systems. These operating functions are listed below in the form of critical questions.

Core Operating Functions
- *Provide Conceptual Clarity.* Is there a clear and generally shared idea of what is meant by prevention?
- *Policy Development.* Have clear policies supporting prevention been enacted by various policy groups?
- *Strategic Planning.* Is there a coordinated strategic planning effort for prevention in place?
- *Evaluation.* Is there a coordinated effort to evaluate the results of existing prevention work and share findings?
- *Federal/State/Local Collaboration.* Are there specific channels through which state and federal level resources coordinate to support local prevention work?
- *Training and Technical Assistance.* Is there an organized system of training and technical assistance available to support prevention work at all levels?
- *Resource Commitment.* Is there an ongoing commitment to allocate funding and other resources to effectively support prevention work?
- *Program Models.* Are there clear prevention models and frameworks that people can use to guide their prevention work?
- *Data Base.* Is there an available, consistent data base that is being used for prevention planning?
- *Leadership Development.* Are there identifiable advocates for prevention in the system who are recognized as prevention leaders and who promote leadership development in others?
- *Educational Support.* Do the educational institutions which train helping professionals of the community and provide continuing education for them have a demonstrated commitment to prevention?
- *Research.* Is there a commitment to ongoing prevention research and the disseminating of relevant findings?
- *Valuing Culture, Diversity and Inclusion.* Is there a commitment to operationalizing the valuing of culture, diversity and inclusion in all aspects of prevention work?

- *Marketing and Recognizing.* Are there mechanisms in place to provide for recognition of and marketing for credible prevention work?

Functional Areas Within a Community's Prevention Training System

In the development and maintenance of any system there are critical functional areas that are essential to the survival and growth of that system. Following are five core functions of a prevention training system:

Prevention Training System Management. This area includes tasks involved in overall management of the training system. Training systems management is responsible for the development and monitoring of system operations, representation of training to the external world, and overall day-to-day training management. It includes communication and coordination with other state agencies providing prevention training services, prevention service providers, and local community coalitions, negotiation of the scheduling and content of training, and overall supervision of training services.

This area also involves the coordination of all training services, including trainer/consultant scheduling, site selection and coordination, participant registration, course record-keeping, consultant contracting, agency and program file maintenance and report preparation.

Curriculum Development. This area includes overall curriculum planning to ensure that skills taught through training are responsive to the evolving needs of communities implementing prevention strategies. It oversees the development of courses that are reflective of comprehensive prevention strategy and the integration of training courses offered within a skill area to ensure mastery of those skills. Curriculum development focuses on content research, training course design and development, materials development, and course revisions and modification.

Theory and Research. This area includes research and study of current practices in fields related to prevention and social change. It includes research in such areas as prevention, systems theory, training, adult learning theory, etc. The function of this area is to ensure the timely transfer of current prevention knowledge and practice to the skill development process of those working in the field.

Trainer/Staff Development. This area consists of skill-related needs assessment for trainer/staff development; recruitment, orientation and development of trainers; design and implementation of general and course-specific trainer development programs; trainer observation; and individual trainer skill assessment.

Reforming the Media. Public and private sector joint initiatives are needed to train a new generation of communication and media, specialists who can articulate policies and programs that do work in the substance abuse field.

Evaluation. This area includes the development of instruments and processes to assist in the planning and development of curriculum, the development of trainers, as well as the implementation of training itself. Evaluation provides a lens through which to assess the needs of the community system in implementing the prevention strategies and specifically the skills necessary to implement those strategies. Its critical focus is on assessing whether the knowledge and skill development introduced through training are transferred to successful application in the community.

Conclusion

It will take both the Boys on the Hill in Washington, D.C., and the Boys in the Hood, to impact outcome-based systems change. As John Gardner warned, grass-roots organizations and citizen-action groups must be prepared to make sacrifices for the purpose of making a difference. The greatness and durability of most civilizations has been finally determined by how they have responded to challenges from within. Just how America will respond to the challenge of systems change is too soon to tell.

Bibliography

Introduction

Curtis, Lynn A. (1995). The state of families. Milwaukee, WI: Families International, Inc.

Chapter 1

Abbey, A., Smith, M.J., and Scott, R.O. (1993). The relationship between reasons for drinking alcohol and alcohol consumption: An interactional Approach. *Addictive Behaviors.* 18 (6): 659-670.

Akbar, N., Saafir, R.K., and Granberry-Stewart, D. (1980). Community psychology and systems intervention. In L. Ramey (Ed.), *Readings for Mental Health and Human Service Workers in the Black Community.* Atlanta: Southern Regional Education Board.

Alvy, K.T. (1991). Parent training as a prevention strategy. In OSAP's *Parent Training is Prevention: Preventing Alcohol and Other Drug Problems Among Youth in the Family.* Washington, D.C.: DHHS Publication No. (ADM) 91-1715.

Amuleru-Marshall, O. (1990). Prevention models for black youth at high risk: Family and religion. In U.J. Oyemade and D. Brandon-Monye

(Eds.), *Ecology of Alcohol and Other Drug Use: Helping Black High-Risk Youth*. Rockville, MD: DHHS Publication No. (ADM) 90-1692.

Amuleru-Marshall, O. (1992). Nurturing the black adolescent male: Culture, ethnicity, and race. In L.W. Abramczyk and J.W. Ross. (Eds.), *Nurturing the Black Adolescent Male in the Family Context: A Public Health Responsibility*. Columbia, SC: The University of South Carolina College of Social Work.

Amuleru-Marshall, O. (1993). Political and economic implications of alcohol and other drugs in the African American community. In L.L. Goddard (Ed.), *An African-Centered Model of Prevention for African-American Youth at High Risk*. Rockville, MD: CSAP Technical Report 6, DHHS Publication No. (SMA) 93-2015.

Amuleru-Marshall, O. (In press). African Americans. In J. Kinney (Ed.), *Clinical Manual of Substance Abuse*. St. Louis, MO: Mosby Year Book, Inc.

Bell, G.D. (1969). Formality versus flexibility in complex organizations. In F.D. Carver and T.J. Sergiovanni (Eds.), *Organizations and Human Behavior: Focus on Schools*. New York: McGraw Hill Book Company.

Biddle, W.W., and Biddle, W.J. (1965). *The Community Development Process: The Rediscovery of Local Initiative*. New York: Holt, Rinehart and Winston, Inc.

Blau, P.M., and Scott, W.R. (1969). The nature and types of formal organizations. In F.D. Carver and T.J. Sergiovanni (Eds.), *Organizations and Human Behavior: Focus on Schools*. New York: McGraw Hill Book Company.

Bulhan, H.A. (1985). *Frantz Fanon and the Psychology of Oppression*. New York: Plenum Press.

Catalano, R.F., Howard, M.O., Hawkins, J.D., and Wells, E.A. (1988). Relapse in the addictions: rates, determinants, and promising relapse prevention strategies. Paper prepared for *The Surgeon General's*

Report. *The Health Consequences of Smoking: Nicotine Addiction.* Washington, D.C.: Office of Smoking and Health.

Center for Substance Abuse Prevention (1993). Individual risk and protective factors. In CSAP Technical Report: *Prevention Strategies Based on Individual Risk Factors for Alcohol and Other Drug Abuse.* Rockville, MD: DHHS Publication No (ADM) 1996-93.

Cooper, M.L., Peirce, R.S., and Huselid, R.F. (1994). Substance use and sexual risk-taking among black adolescents and white adolescents. *Health Psychology.* 13 (3): 251-262.

Continental Congress. (1776). *The Declaration of Independence.*

Edwards, G., Anderson, P., Babor, T.F., Casswell, S., Ferrence, R., Giesbrecht, N., Godfrey, C., Holder, H.D., Lemmens, P., Ma'kela', K., Midanik, L.T., Norstrom, T., Osterberg, E., Romelsjo', A., Room, R., Simpura, J. and Skog, O. (1994). *Alcohol Policy and the Public Good.* New York: Oxford University Press.

Groves, G., and Amuleru-Marshall, O. (1994). Chemical use and dependency among African Americans. In I.L. Livingston (Ed.), *Handbook of Black American Health: The Mosaic of Conditions Issues Policies, and Prospects.* Westport, CT: Greenwood Press.

Hawkins, J.D., Lishner, D.M., Jenson, J.M., and Catalano, R.F. (1990). Delinquents and drugs: What the evidence suggests about prevention and treatment programming. In B.S. Brown and A.R. Mills (Eds.), *Youth at High Risk for Substance Abuse.* Rockville, MD: DHHS Publication No. (ADM) 90-1537.

Hilliard, A.G. (1986). A review of Cheikh Anta Diop's *The Cultural Unity of Black Africa: The Domains of Patriarchy and of Matriarchy in Classical Antiquity.* In I. Van Sertima and L. Williams (Eds.), *Great African Thinkers Vol. I.* New Brunswick: Transaction Books.

Johnson, C.A. (1986). Prevention and control of substance abuse. In J.M. Last (Ed.), *Public Health and Preventive Medicine.* Norwalk, CT: Appleton-Century-Crofts.

Karenga, M. (1989). *Introduction to Black Studies*. University of Sankore Press.

Landis, J.R. (1992). *Sociology: Concepts and Characteristics*. Belmont, CA: Wadsworth Publishing Company.

Last, J.M. (1992). Scope and methods of prevention. In J.M. Last and R.B. Wallace (Eds.), *Public Health and Preventive Medicine*. East Norwalk, CT: Appleton and Lange.

Last, J.M. (1986). Scope and methods of prevention. In J.M. Last (Ed.), *Public Health and Preventive Medicine*. Norwalk, CT: Appleton-Century-Crofts.

Maguire, K., and Pastore, A.L. (Eds.) (1994). *Sourcebook of Criminal Justice Statistics 1993*. Washington, D.C.: U.S. Department of Justice.

Maibach, E.W., Kreps, G.L., and Bonaguro, E.W. (1993). Developing strategic communication campaigns for HIV/AIDS prevention. In S.C. Ratzan (Ed.), *AIDS: Effective Health Communication for the 90s*. Washington, D.C.: Taylor and Francis.

Manley, M. (1974). *The Politics of Change: A Jamaican Testament*. London: Andre Deutsch Limited.

Mann, P.A. (1978). *Community Psychology: Concepts and Applications*. New York: The Free Press.

McLeroy, K.R., Steckler, A.B., Simons-Morton, B., Goodman, R.M., Gottlieb, N., and Burdine, J.N. (1993). Social science theory in health education: Time for a new model. *Health Education Research*. 8 (3): 305-312.

National Cancer Institute (1989). *Making Health Communication Programs Work: A Planners Guide*. Bethesda, MD: NIH Publication No. 89-1493.

National Center for Health Statistics. (1990). *Vital Satistics of the United States*. Washington, D.C.: U.S. Government Printing Office.

Nobles, W. (1985). Africanity and the black family: Development of a theoretical model. Oakland, CA: Black Family Institute.

Nobles, W., and Goddard, Lawford. (1993). Understanding the black family: A guide for scholarship and research. Oakland, CA: Black Family Institute.

Pierce, C.M. (1970). Offense mechanism. In F. Barbour (Ed.), *The Black 70s*. Boston, MA: Porter Sargent.

Rappaport, Julian. (1977). Terms of empowerment/exemplars of prevention: Toward a theory for community psychology. *American Journal of Community Psychology* 15 (2): 121-144.

Singer, M. (1995). Providing substance abuse treatment to Puerto Rican clients living in the continental United States. In O. Amuleru-Marshall (Ed.), *Substance Abuse treatment in the Era of AIDS Vol. II*. Rockville, MD: Center for Substance Abuse Treatment.

Task Force on Alcohol and Drugs. (1987). Substance use, misuse, and dependency. *Journal of American College Health*. 36: 60-63.

Taylor, R.B., Denham, J.W., and Ureda, J.R. (1982). Health promotion: A perspective. In R.B. Taylor, J.W. Denham, and J.R. Ureda (Eds.), *Health Promotion: Principles and Clinical Applications*. Norwalk, CT: Appleton-Century-Crofts.

Wallack, L., Dorfman, L., Jernigan, D., and Themba, M. (1993). *Media Advocacy and Public Health: Power for Prevention*. Newbury Park, CA: Sage.

Chapter 2

Bachman, J.G., Johnston, L.D., and O'Malley, P.M. (1987). *Monitoring the Future: Questionnaire Responses from the Nation's High School Seniors*. Ann Arbor: University of Michigan.

Bachman, J., Johnston, L., and O'Malley, P. (1991). How changes in drug use are linked to perceived risks and disapproval: Evidence from national studies that youth and young adults respond to information about the consequences of drug use. In L. Donohew, H. Sypher, and W. Bukoski (Eds.), *Persuasive Communication and Drug Abuse Prevention*. Hillside, NJ: Lawrence Erlbaum Associates, 133-155.

Bangert-Drowns, R. (1988). The effects of school-based substance abuse education: A meta-analysis. *Journal of Drug Education*. 18 (3): 243-264.

Bosworth, K., and Sailes, J. (1993). Content and teaching strategies in ten selected drug abuse prevention curricula. *Journal of School Health*. 63 (6): 247-253.

Botvin, G., Baker, E., Filazolla, A., and Botvin, E. (1990). A cognitive behavioral approach to substance abuse prevention: One year follow-up. *Addictive Behaviors*. 15: 47-63.

Botvin, G. (1990). Substance abuse prevention: Theory, practice and effectiveness. In M. Tonry and J. Wilson (Eds.), *Drugs and Crime* (Crime and Justice, Vol. 11, pp. 461-520). Chicago, IL: University of Chicago Press.

Botvin, G. (in press). *Life Skills Training*. New Jersey: Princeton Health Press.

Brown, J. and Caston, M. D'Emidio. (In press). On becoming "at risk" through drug education: How symbolic polices and their practices affect students. *Evaluation Review*.

Chaney, B., and Farris, E. (1987). *Report to Congress on the Nature and Effectiveness of Federal, State, and Local Drug Prevention/*

Education Programs. Part 4: Prevention Activities of State Education Agencies. Washington, D.C.: U.S. Department of Education, October 1987.

Chaney, B., Farris, E., and Westat, Inc. (1988). Prevention activities of state education agencies. *Report to Congress on the nature and effectiveness of federal, state, and local drug prevention/education programs. Part 4* (Department of Education, Office of Planning, Budget and Evaluation, pp. 1-19). Washington, D.C.: U.S. Government Printing Office.

Connell, D., Turner, R., and Mason, F. (1985). Summary of findings of the School Health Education Evaluation: Health promotion effectiveness, implementation, and costs. *Journal of School Health.* 55 (8): 316-321.

Ennett, S., Tobler, N., Ringwalt, C., and Flewelling, R. (1994). How effective is drug abuse resistance education? A meta-analysis of Project DARE outcome evaluation. *American Journal of Public Health.* 84 (9): 1394-1401.

Fowler, W., and Walberg, H. (Summer, 1991). School size, characteristics, and outcomes. *Educational Evaluation and Policy Evaluation.* 13 (2): 189-202.

Goldstein, Arnold. (1993). Gang intervention: A historical review. In A. Goldstein and C.R. Huff (Eds.), *The Gang Intervention Handbook.* Champaign, IL: Research Press, 21-51.

Hansen, W. (1992). School-based substance abuse prevention: A review of the art in curriculum, 1980-1990. *Health Education Research.* 7 (3): 403-430.

Hopkins, R., Mauss, A., Kearney, K., and Weisheit, R. (1988). Comprehensive evaluation of a model alcohol curriculum. *Journal of Studies on Alcohol.* 49 (1): 38-50.

Johnston, L., O'Malley, P., and Bachman, J. (1995). National survey results on drug use from *The Monitoring the Future Study, 1975-*

1994, Volume 1, Secondary School Students (NIH Publication No. 95-4026). Washington, D.C.: U.S. Government Printing Office.

Klitzner, M.D. (1987). *Report to Congress on the Nature and Effectiveness of Federal, State, and Local Drug Prevention/Education Programs. Part 2: An Assessment of the Research on School-Based Prevention Programs*. Washington, D.C.: U.S. Department of Education, October 1987.

McGeary, G.H. (1988). *Inner City Poverty in the US.* Washington, D.C.: National Academy Press.

NIDA Capsule C-84-3, Revised August 1989.

Rosenthal, R. (1994). Parametric measures of effect size. In H. Cooper and L. Hedges (Eds.), *The Handbook of Research Synthesis*. New York: Russell Sage Foundation, 231-144.

Tobler, N., and Stratton, H. (In press). Effectiveness of school-based drug prevention programs: A meta-analysis of the research. *The Journal of Primary Prevention.* 17(3).

Chapter 3

American Psychological Association. (1993). *Violence and Youth: Psychology's Response*. Washington, D.C.

A Survey of Experiences, Perceptions and Apprehensions About Guns Among Young People in America. (1993). New York: Louis Harris and Associates, Inc., and LH Research, Inc.

Allen-Hagen, B., Sickmund, M., and Snyder, H. (1994). *Juveniles and Violence: Juvenile Offending and Victimization*. Fact Sheet #19. Washington, D.C.: U.S. Department of Justice, Office of Juvenile Justice and Delinquency Prevention.

Block, Carolyn B. (1985). *Lethal Violence in Chicago over Seventeen Years: Homicides Known to the Police 1965-1981.* Statistical Analysis Center, Illinois Criminal Justice Information Authority.

Block, Carolyn B., Block, Rebecca, and Block, Richard. (1993). Street gang crime in Chicago. *Research in Brief.* National Institute of Justice, Office of Justice Programs, U.S. Department of Justice.

Blumstein, A. (1994). *Youth, Violence, Guns, and the Illicit-Drug Industry.* Pittsburgh, PA: Carnegie Mellon University.

Blumstein, A., Cohen, J., Roth, J.A., and Visher, C.A. (1986). *Criminal Careers and Career Criminals.* Washington D.C.: National Academy of Science Press.

Bourgois, P. (1987). In search of Horatio Alger: Culture and ideology in the crack economy. *Contemporary Problems.* 16 (winter):619-649.

Burns, T.F. (1980). Getting rowdy with the boys. *Journal of Drug Issues.* 10: 273-286.

Bursik, Robert J., Jr. (1988). Social disorganization and theories of crime and delinquency: Problems and prospects. *Criminology.* 26 (4): 519-551.

Centers for Disease Control. (1986). *Homicide Surveillance: High Risk Racial and Ethnic Groups—Blacks and Hispanics, 1970-1983.* Atlanta, GA: CDC.

Centers for Disease Control. (1991). Forums on youth violence in minority communities 1990. *Public Health Reports.* 106 (3):225-277. Rockville, MD.

Chaiken, J., and Chaiken, M. (1990). Drugs and predatory crime. In M. Tonry and J.Q. Wilson (Eds.), *Drugs and Crime.* Chicago: University of Chicago Press.

Cohen, M.A. (1994). *The Monetary Value of Saving a High-Risk Youth.* Washington, D.C.: The Urban Institute.

Curry, G. David, and Spergel, Irving A. (1988). Gang homicide, delinquency, and community. *Criminology*. 26 (August): 381-405.

Curry, G. David, and Spergel, Irving A. (1992). Gang involvement and delinquency among Hispanic and African-American adolescent males. *Journal of Research in Crime and Delinquency*. 29 (3): 273-292.

Curry, G. David, Fox, Robert J., Ball, Richard A., and Stone, Darryl. (1992). *National Assessment of law Enforcement Anti-Gang Information Resources*. (Draft 1992 Final Report). Morgantown, WV.

Curtis, L.A. (1975). *Violence, Race and Culture.* Lexington, MA: D.C. Heath.

Fagan, Jeffrey. (1987). Neighborhood education, mobilization and organization for juvenile prevention. *Annals of the American Academy of Political and Social Services*. 494 (November): 55-70.

Fagan, Jeffrey. (1989). The social organization of drug use and drug dealing among urban gangs. *Criminology* 27 (4): 633-699.

Fagan, J., and Wexler, Sandy. (1987) Family origins of violent delinquents. *Criminology* 25 (3): 643-669.

Fagan, J., Piper, E., and Moore, M. (1986). Violent delinquents and urban youth. *Criminology* 24 (3): 439-471.

Federal Bureau of Investigation. (1995). *Uniform Crime Reports for the United States 1995: A National Crime Survey*. Washington D.C.: U.S. Department of Justice.

Felson, R.B., and Steadman, H.J. (1983). Situational factor in disputes leading to criminal violence. *Criminology*. 21: 59-74.

Feyerherm, W., Pope, C., and Lovell, R. (1992). *Youth Gang Prevention and Early Intervention Programs and Final Research Report*. Washington, D.C.: U.S. Department of Justice, Office of Juvenile Justice and Delinquency Prevention.

Fingerhut, L., Klienman, E., Godfrey E., and Rosenberg, R. (1991). Firearm mortality among children, youth and young adults 1-34 years of age: Trends and current status. United States 1979-1988. *CDC/ NCHS Monthly Vital statistics Reports.* 39 (11 supplemental). Hyattsville, MD.

Garafalo, J., Siegel, L., and Laub, J. (1987). School related victimization among adolescents: An analysis of National Crime Survey Narrative. *Journal of Quantitative Criminology.* 3:321-338.

Goldstein, Arnold. (1993). Gang intervention: A historical review. In A. Goldstein and C.R. Huff (Eds.), *The Gang Intervention Handbook.* Champaign, IL: Research Press, 21-51.

Goldstein, Arnold P., Carthon, Wilam, and Blancero, Douglas. (1994). *The Prosocial Gang.* Thousand Oaks, CA: Sage.

Goldstein, Henry. (1990). *Problem-Oriented Policing.* Philadelphia, PA: Temple University Press.

Goldstein, Paul. (1985). The drugs/violence nexus: A tripartite conceptual framework. *Journal of Drug Issues.* Fall: 493-506.

Goldstein, P.J. (1982). Drugs and crime. In M. Wolfgang and N.A. Wiener (Eds.), *Pathways to Criminal Violence.* Beverly Hills, CA: Sage.

Goldstein, P.J. (1989). Crack and homicide in NYC, 1988. *Contemporary Drug Problems.* 16 (winter): 651-687.

Griffin, E.H., and Bell, C.C. (1989). Recent trends in suicide and homicide among blacks. A special communication. *Journal of the American Medical Association.* 282 (16): 2265-2269.

Hagedorn, John. (1992). Gangs, neighborhoods, and public policy. *Social Problems.* 38 (4): 529-542.

Hamid, A. (1990). The political economy of crack related violence. *Contemporary Drug Problems.* 17 (spring): 31-78.

Bibliography

Harris, Mary. (1988). *Cholas: Latino girls and gangs.* New York: AMS.

Horowitz, Ruth. (1983). Community tolerance of gang violence. *Social Problems.* 34 (5): 437-450.

Howell, J.C. (Ed.) (1995). *Guide for Implementing the Comprehensive Strategy for Serious, Chronic and Violent, and Chronic Juvenile Offenders.* Washington, D.C.: U.S. Department of Justice, Office of Juvenile Justice and Delinquency Prevention.

Jagger, J., and Dietz, P.E. (1987). Deaths and injury by firearms. *Journal of Trauma.* 27: 532-536.

Jencks, C., and Meyers, S. (1990). The social consequences of growing up in a poor neighborhood. In L.E. Lynn and G.H. McGeary (Eds.), *Inner City Poverty in the U.S.* Washington, D.C.: National Academy Press.

Johnson, B., et al. (1990). Drug abuse in the inner city: Impact on hard drugs and the community. In M. Tonry and J.Q. Wilson (Eds.), *Drugs and Crime.* Chicago: University of Chicago Press.

Kellerman, A.L., and Reay, D.T. (1988). Protection or peril? An analysis of firearm related deaths in the home. *New England Journal of Medicine.* 319: 1256-1266.

Kellerman, A.L., Lee, R.K., Mercey, J.A., and Banton, J. (1991). The epidemiological basis for the prevention of firearms injuries. *The Annual Review of Public Health.* 12: 17-40.

Klien, Malcolm W. (1969). Violence in American juvenile gangs. In D.J. Mulvihill, M.M. Tumin, and L.A. Curtis. *Crime of Violence Series, Vol. 13.* National Commission the Causes and Prevention of Violence. Washington, D.C.: U.S. Government Printing Office, 1427-1460.

Klien, Malcolm W. (1992). *Twenty-five Years of Youth Gangs and Violence.* Social Science Research Institute. Los Angeles: University of Southern California.

Klien, Malcolm W., and Maxson, Cheryl L. (1987). Street gang violence. In M.E. Wolfgang and N. Weiner (Eds.), *Violent Crime, Violent Criminals*. Beverly Hills, CA: Sage.

Klien, M., Maxson, C.L., and Cunningham, L. (1988). *Gang Involvement in Rock Trafficking*. NIJ Final Report. Washington, D.C.: NIJ.

Kraus, J., Sorenson, S.B., and Juarez, P. (1987). *Research Conference on Violence and Homicide in Hispanic Communities*. Los Angeles, CA: UCLA.

Maxson, Cheryl L., Gordon, Margaret A., and Klien, Malcolm W. (1985). Differences between gang and non-gang homicides. *Criminology* 23: 209-222.

McGeary, G.H. (1988). *Inner City Poverty in the US*. Washington, D.C.: National Academy Press.

Mercey, James, and O Carroll P.W. (1988). New directions in violence prediction: The public health arena. *Violence and Victims*. 3 (4): 285-301.

Mercey, James, and Houck, V.N. (1988). Firearm injuries: A call for science. *New England Journal of Medicine* 319 (19): 1283-1285.

Mieczkowski, T. (1989). The operational styles of crackhouses in Detroit. Paper NIDA Technical review panel on Drugs and Violence, Rockville, MD.

Morales, Armando. (1989). Urban gang violence: A psychological crisis. In Armando Morales and Bradford W. Sheafer (Eds.), *Social Work: A Profession of Many Faces*. Boston: Allyn and Bacon, Inc., 605-613, 620-630.

Musto, D. (1973). *The American Disease*. New Haven, CT: Yale University Press.

National Research Council. (1993). *Understanding and Preventing Violence.* NAS/National Research Council. Washington D.C.: National Academy Press.

Riess, Albert, and Roth, Jeffrey. (1993). *Understanding and Controlling Violence.* Report of the National Academy of Sciences Panel on the Understanding and Control of Violence. Washington, D.C.: National Academy Press.

Rosenberg, M.L. (1990). Violence is a public health problem. In R.C. Maulitz (Ed.), *Unnatural Causes: The Three Leading Killer Diseases in America.* New Brunswick, N.J.: Rutgers University Press.

Rosenberg, J., and Fenley, M. (1991). *Violence in America: A Public Health Approach.* New York City: Oxford Press.

Ruttenburg, H. (1994). The limited promise of public health methodologies to prevent youth violence. *The Yale Law Journal* 103: 1885.

Saltzman, L.E., Mercey, J., Rosenberg, J., et al. (1990). Magnitude and patterns of family and intimate violence in Atlanta, Georgia, 1984. *Violence and Victims.* 5 (1): 3-17.

Sampson, R. (1987). Urban black violence the effect of male joblessness and family disruption. *American Journal of Sociology* 93 (2): 348-382.

Schorr, Lisbeth. (1988). *Within Our Reach.* New York: Doubleday.

Sheley, J.F., Wright, J.D., and McGee, Z.T. (1992). Gun related violence in and around inner-city schools. *American Journal of Diseases of Children* 146 (6): 677-682.

Siberman, C.E. (1978). *Criminal Violence and Criminal Justice.* Vintage Books.

Smith J., Mercey, J., and Rosenberg, J. (1984). *Comparison of Homicide among Anglos and Hispanics in Five Southwestern States.* Paper presented at U.S./Mexico Border Health Meetings, Hermosillio, Mexico.

Snyder, H.M., Sickmund, M., and Poe-Yamagata, E. (1996). *Juvenile Offenders and Victims: 1996 Update on Violence.* Washington, D.C: U.S. Department of Justice, Office of Juvenile Justice and Delinquency Prevention.

Spergel, Irving A. (1986). The violent gang in Chicago: a local community approach. *Social Service Review* 60 (March).

Spergel, Irving A. (1992). Youth gangs: an essay review. *Social Service Review* 6 (1): 121-140.

Spergel, Irving A., and Curry, G. David, with Ross, Ruth E., and Chance, Ron L. (1990). *Survey of Youth Gang Problems and Programs in 45 Cities and 6 Sites.* Chicago: University of Chicago, School of Social Service Administration.

Spergel, I. (1995). *The Youth Gang Problem: A Community Approach.* New York: Oxford University Press.

Taylor, Carl S. (1988). Youth gangs organize for power, money. *School Safety.* Spring: 26-27.

Tobler, N., and Stratton, H. (In press). Effectiveness of school-based drug prevention programs: A meta-analysis of the research. *The Journal of Primary Prevention.* 17(3).

Tolan, P., and Guerra, N. (1994). *What Works in Reducing Adolescent Violence: An Empirical Review of the Field.* Boulder, CO: Center for the Study and Prevention of Violence, University of Colorado.

Tonry, M., and Wilson, J.Q. (1990). *Drugs and Crime.* Chicago: University of Chicago Press.

U.S. Department of Health and Human Services (DHHS). *Health of the United States: 1999.* Hyattville, MD: Public Health Service.

170 Bibliography

U.S. Department of Justice (DOJ)/NIJ. *Criminal Victimization in the United States 1999: A National Crime Survey.* Washington D.C.: Bureau of Justice Assistance, U.S. Department of Justice.

Waldorf, Dan. (1993). *When the CRIPS Invaded San Francisco—Gang Migration, Home Boy Study.* Alameda, CA: Institute for Scientific Analysis.

Wilson, William J. (1991). Public policy research and the truly disadvantaged. In C. Jencks and P.E. Peterson (Eds.), *The Urban Underclass.* Washington, D.C.: The Brookings Institute, 460-481.

Wilson, John, and Howell, James. (1993). *A Comprehensive Strategy for Serious, Violent and Chronic Juvenile Offenders.* Washington, D.C.: U.S. Department of Justice, Office of Juvenile Justice and Delinquency Prevention.

Wintemute, G.J., Teret, S.P., Kraus, J.F., and Wright, M.A. (1992). When children shoot children: 88 unintentional deaths. *Journal of the American Medical Association.* :3107-3109.

Wish, E., and Johnson, B.D. (1986). The impact of substance abuse on criminal careers. In A. Blumstein, J. Cohen, J.A. Roth, C.A. Visher (Eds.), *Criminal Careers and Career Criminals.* Washington, D.C.: National Academy of Science Press.

Wolfgang, M., and Wiener, N.A. (1982). *Criminal Violence.* Beverly Hills, CA: Sage.

Zimring, F.E. (1986). Gun control. *Bulletin of the New York Academy of Medicine.* 62: 615-621.

Zimring, F.E. (1989). The problem of assault firearms. *Crime and Delinquency.* 35 (4): 538-545.

Zimring, F.E. (1991). Firearms, violence and public policy. *The Scientific American.* November: 48-54.

Chapter 5

Butterfoss, F., Goodman, R., and Wandersman, A. (1993). Community coalitions for prevention and health promotion. *Health Education Research: Theory and Practice.* 8.

Cook, R., Roehl, J., Oro, C., and Trudeau, J. (In press). Conceptual and methodological issues in the evaluation of community based substance abuse prevention coalitions; Lessons learned in the national evaluation of the community partnership program. *Journal of Community Psychology.*

CSAP. (1991). *CSAP's Foundation Initiative Strategic Plan.* Rockville, MD: Center for Substance Abuse Prevention.

Gerstein, D., and Green, L. (1993). *Preventing Drug Abuse, What Do We Know?* Washington, D.C.: National Academy Press.

Green, Lawrence, W. (1986). The theory of participation: A qualitative analysis of its expression in national and international health policies. *Advances in Health Education and Promotion, Vol. 1., Pt. A.* JAI Press, 21-236.

Health and Welfare Canada. (1986). *Achieving Health for All: National Framework for Health Promotion.* Ottawa, Ontario.

Prevention in Perspective (1990). Washington, D.C.: National Association of State Alcohol and Drug Abuse Directors.

Puska, P., Nissinen, A., Salonen, J.T., Tuomileheto, J. (1983). Ten years of North Karilia Project: Results with community based prevention of coronary heart disease. *Scandinavian Journal of Social medicine.* 11:65-68.

Stunkard, A.J., Felix, M.R.J., Cohen R.Y. (1985). Mobilizing communities to promote health: The Pennsylvania County Health Improvement Program. In J.C. Rosen and L.J. Solomon (Eds.), *Prevention In Health Psychology.* Hanover: University Press of New England.

Bibliography

Tarlov, A.R., et al. (1987). Foundation work: The health promotion program of the Henry J. Kaiser Family Foundation. *American Journal of Health Promotion.* 2 (2).

Tarlov, A.R., and Felix, M.R.J. (In press). *The Production of Health in America: Mobilizing Communities.* Oxford Press.

U.S. Department of Health, Education, and Welfare. (1979). *Health People: the Surgeon General's Report on Health Promotion and Disease Prevention.* Washington, D.C.: Government Printing Office.

U.S. Department of Health and Human Services. (1991). *Healthy People 2000: National Health Promotion and Disease Prevention Objectives.* DHHS Publication No. (PHS) 91-50212, Washington, D.C.: Superintendent of Documents, U.S. Government Printing Office.

World Health Organization (1978). Alma-Ata 1978. Primary Health Care: Report the International Conference on Primary Health Care, Alma-ATA. USSR, 6-12 September, 1978. Geneva "Health for All" Series, No. 1.

Chapter 6

Cunningham, M.S. (1993). Evaluating alcohol and other drug abuse programs. In E.M. Freeman (Ed.), *Substance Abuse Treatment: A Family Systems Perspective.* Newbury Park, CA: Sage, 267-294.

Freeman, E.M., and Pennekamp, M. (1988). Joining multicultural communities: Building on the positive effects of pluralism. In *Social Work Practice: Toward a Child, Family, School. Community Perspective.* Springfield, IL: Charles C. Thomas Publisher, 99-117.

Freeman, E.M., and O'Dell, K. (1993). Helping communities redefine self-sufficiency from the person-in-environment perspective. *Journal of Intercultural Relations.* 10: 38-53.

Freire, P. (1989). *Pedagogy of the Oppressed.* New York: Continuum.

Guiterrez, L., and Ortega, R. (1991). Developing methods to empower Latinos: The importance of groups. *Social Work with Groups*. 14: 23-43.

Hasselkus, B.R. (1988). Meaning in family caregiving: Perspectives on caregiver/professional relationships. *The Gerontologist*. 28: 686-691.

Hawkins, J.D., and Catalano, R.F. (1992). *Communities that Care*. San Francisco: Jossey-Bass.

Kane, T.J. (1987). Giving back control: Long-term poverty and motivation. *Social Service Review*. 405-419.

LaRossa, R., and Worf, Hane H. (1985). On qualitative family research. *Journal of Marriage and the Family*. 47 (3): 531-541.

Marshall, Catherine, and Rossman, Gretchen B. (1989). *Designing Qualitative Research*. Newbury Park, CA: Sage.

McCracken, S. (1988). *The Long Interview*. Newbury Park, CA: Sage.

Patton, M.Q. (1980). *Qualitative Evaluation Methods*. Beverly Hills, CA: Sage.

Schon, D.A. (1983). *The Reflective Practitioner*. New York: Basic Books, Inc.

Spradley, J. (1979). *The Ethnographic Interview*. New York: Holt, Rinehart, and Winston.

Taylor, S.J., and Bogdan, R. (1984). *Introduction to Qualitative Research Methods*. New York: John Wiley and Sons.

Yeich, S., and Levine, R. (1992). Participatory research's contribution to a conceptualization of empowerment. *Journal of Applied Social Psychology*. 22: 1894-1908.

Chapter 7

Fighting Back National Program Office. (1996). Robert Wood Foundation Mission Statement. Nashville, TN.

Gensheimer, Leah. (1995). Evaluation of Kansas City's Project Neighborhood's Mobilizer Initiative.

Gordon, Jacob U. (1995). *Project SAVE*. Kansas City, MO: Project Neighborhood.

Heimovics, Catherine. (1993). *Baseline Indicators*. Kansas City, MO: University of Missouri in Kansas City.

Kansas City Globe. December 8-14, 1995.

Project Neighborhood. (1990). Community Needs Assessment. Kansas City, MO.

Kansas City Star. May 19, 1996.

U.S. Department of Justice. (1994). *Understanding Community Policing*. Washington, D.C.: Bureau of Justice Assistance (BJA).

Chapter 8

California Department of Alcohol and Drug Programs. (1995). *Prevention Tactics—Policy Panels for Prevention*. 1 (2), June/July.

Jellinek, Paul S., and Hearn, Ruby P. (1991). Fighting drug abuse at the local level. *Issues in Science and Technology, Vol. 7, No. 4*. Washington, D.C.: National Academy of Sciences.

Join Together. (1995). Community Exchange: First year retrospective. September.

Join Together. (1995). Join Together Policy Panel on youth access to alcohol—Creating good public policy: A kit. Summer.

Join Together. (1996). Leading from the ground up—The Third Survey of the community movement against substance abuse. January.

Join Together. (1993). 1993 report to the nation—Community leaders speak out against substance abuse. Summer.

Join Together. (1995). Planning and convening public policy panels. Join Together report.

Join Together. (1994). Strategies. Vol. 3, No. 2. Summer.

Join Together. (1994). Technical assistance for community coalitions—A Join Together report. May.

Join Together. (1992). Who is really fighting the war on drugs? May.

Chapter 10

King Jr., Martin Luther. (1968). *Where Do We Go From Here? Chaos or Community.* Boston, MA: Beacon Press.

Appendices

Appendix A: Definition of Terms
Appendix B: Methodology: Ethnographic Procedures
Appendix C: Integrating Multiple Systems Change Strategies and Inclusive Research Methods
Appendix D: PNH Involvement in Neighborhood Activities
Appendix E: PNH Knowledge of Resources
Appendix F: PNH Linkages
Appendix G: Kansas City Crime Rate

Appendix A
Definition of Terms

Coalition: Coalition is the central organizing entity made up of individual partnerships, alliances, and collaborations, as well as individual organizations, service providers, community groups, and individuals. The term "coalition" is more broadly used to refer to any single group that is organized and working with other groups for a common goal or purpose. Thus, it is possible for "the Coalition" to have as members multiple "coalitions" from throughout the community/area.

Collaboration: On a community level, collaboration involves the mutual understanding, respect, and cooperation of each of the Coalition members. It involves the sharing of resources, a common vision, and a willingness to be flexible for the good of the community. It also involves a mechanism for successfully resolving conflict. Cultural awareness and competency are the keys to collaboration in our highly diverse communities.

Cost Effectiveness and Cost Benefit: Cost effectiveness is a computation of the cost of producing a desired outcome through a program element or initiative. Cost effectiveness is one critical indicator of the benefits of a community's substance abuse prevention approach and methodology. The indicators of effective prevention may be assessed from a system/community-wide, programmatic, and individual level. Often, a good estimate of the cost of a program is the cumulative value of the financial as well as the in-kind resources expended in the prevention program.

Cultural Competence: A set of academic and interpersonal skills that allow individuals to increase their understanding and appreciation of cultural differences and similarities of, within, among, and between groups. This requires a willingness and ability to draw on community-based values, traditions, and customs, and to work with knowledgeable persons of and from the community in developing focused interventions, communications, and other supports. To foster cultural competence, coalitions can facilitate cross-cultural communication, broaden coalition memberships to include people from all ethnic and cultural backgrounds, and approach solutions to substance abuse problems with greater sensitivity and understanding of individual population differences.

Empowerment: Partnerships and coalitions become empowered to act for the good of individuals and organizations within the community when they have the necessary knowledge and tools to confront the problems attendant on alcohol, tobacco and other drug use and abuse. Empowerment can and does include the exchange of power, influence, and control across the coalition toward the goals of reducing substance abuse problems.

Health Care Reform: Health care reform and prevention are intertwined. Community coalitions offer their public- and private-sector members an opportunity to operate effectively within the current systems of health care and coverage. At the same time, the new coalition programs will be laying the foundation for relating preventive services to the health care systems yet to be established in the nation's communities in response to health care reform.

Prevention: A proactive process that empowers individuals and systems to meet the challenges of life events and transitions by creating and reinforcing conditions that promote healthy behaviors and lifestyles leading to the reduction of disease(s) and substance abuse problems.

Prevention Services: Those endeavors which help to ensure that individuals and systems are empowered to meet the challenges of life events and transitions by creating and reinforcing conditions that promote healthy behaviors and lifestyles leading to the reduction of disease(s) and substance abuse problems.

Service Delivery: In keeping with the nation's new climate of optimizing programs and services, coalitions are encouraged to use up to 50 percent of the new grant funds in such a way as to avoid duplication of efforts and cut waste, leverage new resources to fill gaps in services, and position staff and programs to be helpful to the consumer.

Services Integration: A model of interweaving services instituted in the community through common goals and objectives. It achieves reduced redundancy of services, sharing of services, and where possible, a comprehensive, holistic approach to service delivery in the proposed community.

Systems Approach: A systems approach to prevention views the community and the environment as interconnected parts, each affecting the others and all needing to work together.

Systems Change: System-wide changes can have long-term, positive effects on bettering the health and safety of the community. Systems-wide changes also may involve refinement and strengthening of the individual component or part of the community-wide system. These system-wide changes are to be contrasted with short-term, single-focus programs or one-time events and activities. Working within a prevention continuum, such changes may include policy and legislative change, and strategic changes in the structure or nature of organizations and systems in the community.

Target Communities/Areas: Target communities to be served by the coalition and evaluated will be defined geographically. The boundaries of a community do not have to be congruous with those of an incorporated governmental entity such as a town, city, or county. A community may be a subset of a larger incorporated governmental entity or a combination of several incorporated governmental entities.

Target Populations: For the purposes of this article, a target population is defined as a group of residents of a community/area who are served by the same group of service organizations. Coalition involvement will include all racial, ethnic, gender, age, and cultural groups that live in the defined community. Coalitions should make an effort to include special populations in the community which historically have not been included in past community prevention efforts.

Appendix B
Methodology: Ethnographic Procedures

Purpose	Data Collection	Data Sources	Sampling Strategy
NEEDS ASSESSMENTS (Baseline data, program justification)	Key informant interviews	Ethnographic interview	Purposeful (with snowball technique)
	Community forum	Public testimony, anecdotal experiences, open-ended questions	Purposeful (special interest groups: equal representation)
	Focus groups	Semi-structured group interview guide	Purposeful
PROGRAM EVALUATION Process evaluation	Direct observation	Unstructured observation form	Sample 100% or random sampling with time series design during treatment
	Focus groups	Semi-structured group interview guide	Same as above
Outcome evaluation	Client self-reports	Written records	Same as above, but for pre and post treatment periods
	Direct observation	Pre and post roleplays of clients' problem situations	Same as above
	Practitioner feedback	Ethnographic interviews, case studies/records	Same as above
	Key informants	Ethnographic interviews	Same as above
PRACTICE RESEARCH	Quantitative methods combined	Standardized questionnaires	Random assignment, matched comparison

Appendices 181

Appendix C
Integrating Multiple Systems Change Strategies and Inclusive Research Methods

Multiple Micro and Macro Systems Change Strategies	Ethnographic Research Methods	Outcomes in the Community
Micro Strategies • Education • Assertiveness Training • Problem Solving • Decision Making • Analysis of Personal Risks and Protective Factors • Use of Social Supports **Macro Strategies** • Power Analysis • Advocacy • Community Mobilization/Social Action • Policy Impact Analysis/Change • Coalition Building/Leadership Development • Lobbying/Organizational and Legislative Influence • Program Development • Grant Writing	**Community Members/Researchers-Teams Needs Assessment** • Data collectors • Data analysts • Reactors to findings • Participants • In long-term planning • Key informants **Program Evaluation and Practice Research** • Data collectors • Providers of feedback • Analyzers of other published research • Data analysts • Decision making about program revisions • Disseminators of program evaluation findings • Designers of research	• Transfer of institutional power to community members. • Reduction of risk factors. • Empowerment and ownership from systems change efforts. • Higher levels of self-sufficiency (interdependence rather than dependence economically, politically, socially, and psychologically) (protective factors). • Elimination of policies and structural barriers that maintain power gaps and social problems—e.g., inadequate education, substance abuse, violence, economic deficits.

Appendix D
PNH Involvement in Neighborhood Activities

NRS Items 78-81, 83, and 84: *Please circle if you currently are doing any of the following activities.*

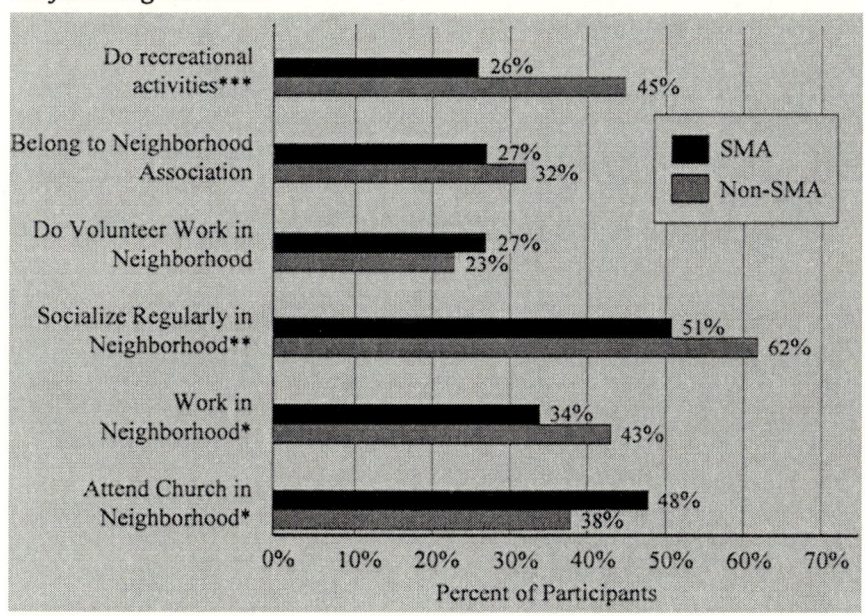

*p < .05; **p < .01; ***p < .001

From: UMKC Department of Psychology, *Evaluation of Project Neighbor-H.O.O.D.'s Mobilizer Initiative, Volume II.*

Appendix E
PNH Knowledge of Resources

NRS Item 41: *Do you know of any people, organizations, or programs that fight drug or alcohol problems in your neighborhood?*

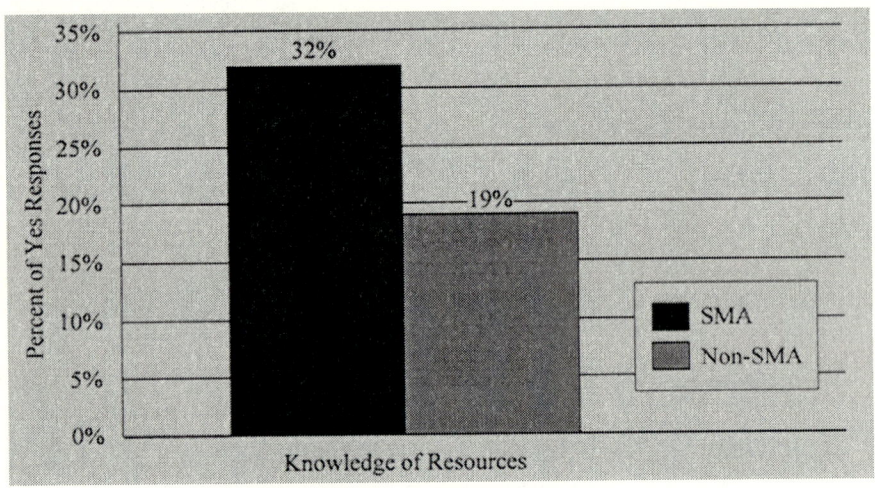

$p < .001$; valid cases = 543

From: UMKC Department of Psychology, *Evaluation of Project Neighbor-H.O.O.D.'s Mobilizer Initiative, Volume II.*

Appendix F
PNH Linkages

Item 238: *Listed below are various audiences or stakeholder groups that you may have worked with in your role as a Mobilizer. Please indicate the* three groups *you worked with* most *often.*

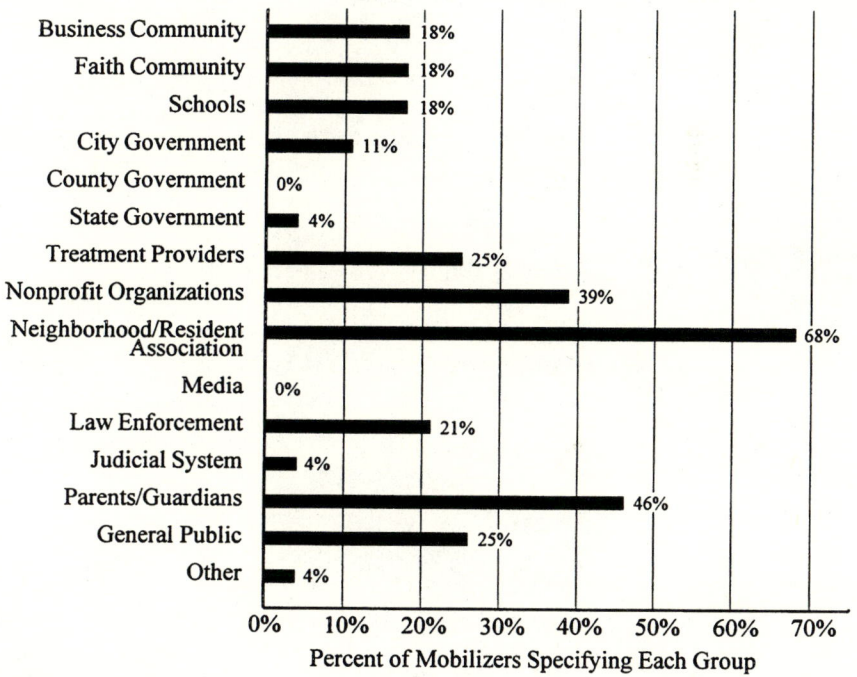

Valid cases = 28
Note: Percentages do not add up to 100% due to multiple responses per participant.

From: UMKC Department of Psychology, *Evaluation of Project Neighbor-H.O.O.D.'s Mobilizer Initiative, Volume II.*

Appendix G
Kansas City Crime Rate

Total Crime Rate

Number of seven most serious crimes, per 1,000 residents, in 1995

1.	Atlanta	174.2
2.	St. Louis	162.2
3.	Miami	159.0
4.	Baltimore	134.9
5.	Tucson, Ariz.	125.9
6.	Portland, Ore.	122.8
7.	Detroit	120.0
8.	Fresno, Calif.	119.7
9.	Washington	119.3
10.	Charlotte, N.C.	119.0
11.	**Kansas City**	**118.4**

Kansas City Murder Rate

Number of murders per 100,000 residents

1992	35.2
1993	35.0
1994	32.9
1995	24.1

1992, 1993, and 1994 rates based on 1992 U.S. census estimates. 1995 rankings and rates based on 1994 census estimates. Crime statistics from FBI's 1995 preliminary report. Based on crime rates for the 50 most populous cities.

Author Index

Alvy, K.T., 4
Amuleru-Marshall, Omowale, xiii, 1-19

Bachman, J.G., 21, 29
Biddle, W.W., 8
Block, Carolyn, 38
Blumstein, A., 33, 38
Botvin, G., 24, 29
Brown, Keith, xiv, 99-121
Bulhan, H.A., 9

Cadet, Tamara, xiv, 123-37
Chaney, B., 22-3, 24
Connell, D., 29
Cook, R., 60
Copple, James, xv, 139-41
Curtis, L.A., 36

Davis, Darlind, xiv, 55-73

Edwards, G., 2, 4
Engstrom, Eric, xiii, 47-53
Ennett, S., 24

Farris, E., 22-3, 24

Felix, Michael, xiv, 55-73
Freeman, Edith, xiv, xv, 75-97, 115, 139, 141-2

Gordon, Jacob U., xi-xv, 115, 147-54
Green, Lawrence, 66
Griffin, E.H., 33, 36
Guiterrez, L., 95, 96

Hasselkus, B.R., 76, 87
Hawkins, 4
Hilliard, A.G., 18
Heimovics, Catherine, 101
Hopkins, R., 24

Jellinek, Paul S., 124
Jencks, C., 35, 36
Johnson, C.A., 2, 3
Johnston, L.D., 21, 29

Kane, T.J., 91
Karenga, M., 9
Keeling, Richard, xiii, 47-53
King, Martin Luther, Jr., 147
Klitzner, M.D., 22

Last, J.M., 2, 4
Larson, Mary Jo, xv, 139, 143-5
Lee, Janine, xv, 139, 142-3

McCracken, S., 77, 85, 87
Manley, Michael, 11, 12, 18
Mann, P.A., 8
Marshall, Catherine, 78, 79, 80, 88
Mata, Alberto, xiii, 33-46
Mercey, James, 33, 37-42

Nobles, 9, 13, 18

O'Dell, Kristi, xiv, 75-97
O'Malley, P.M., 21, 29

Patton, M.W., 76, 85
Pierce, 11

Rappaport, 15-6, 17, 18
Rosenberg, Mark, 37-42
Ryan, William, 15-6, 18

Spergel, Irving A., 34
Spradley, J., 76, 77, 85
Stratton, H., 24

Tarlov, A.R., 57, 68
Taylor, S.J., 78, 79, 82, 84, 85, 86
Tobler, Nancy, xiii, 21-31

Wallack, L., 11, 18

Zimring, F.E., 36, 38

Subject Index

Adolescents:
    health issues, 47-53
    health promotion strategies for, 51-3
    mass media influences, 50-1
    peer pressure, 50-1
    prevention evaluation, 143-5
    school-based drug prevention programs, 21-31
    self-esteem, 49, 50, 52
    styles of learning, 49, 50
    substance abuse, 21, 29, 50
    youth prevention networks, 141-2, 143
    youth task forces (PNH), 139-41
African-Americans, 1, 18
    community, 8-9, 14, 17, 19
    cultural domination of, 9, 17
    education, 15
    exogenous/endogenous systems and, 14
    incarceration, 9, 10
    infant mortality, 15
    morbidity, 9, 10
    mortality rates, 9, 10
    policy making, involvement in, 58
    poverty rate, xii
    unemployment rate, xiii, 15
    urban population, xii
    young homicide rate, 39
Alcoholics Anonymous (AA), 2
Alcohol, tobacco and other drug (ATOD) problems, xiv, xv
    coalition model for reduction, 59, 61-2
    community empowerment, 55, 56, 57, 62, 63, 71
    Community Partnership Program, 64-7
    costs to society, 99
    financial resources, competition for, 56
    health care costs of, 57
    politics and solutions, 55
    prevention, 58, 60
    psychosocial and ecological determinants of, 57
    resources spent on, 68
Alma Ata Declaration, 63
American Psychological Association (APA), 34

Asian-Americans:
  drug-related crime reduction and, 65
  immigrant population, xii
  policy making, involvement in, 58

Brown, Lee, 67

Califano, Joseph, 57
Center for Substance Abuse Prevention (CSAP), 60, 61
  Community Partnership Program, 64-5, 72
  evaluation report, 58-9
  Gloucester Prevention Network, 59
  National Foundation Initiative, 70, 71, 72
  partner foundations, coordination, 69-70
Center on Addiction and Substance Abuse (CASA), 57
Chemical dependence, see alcohol, drug, ATOD, and substance abuse
Cigarettes, adolescent use, 21, 29
Cocaine Anonymous (CA), 2
Community:
  definitions of, 8
  substance abuse prevention, 4-6
Community-based organizations, 35, 36, 40, 41
  Public Health Model approach to violence, 42-5
  violence prevention, 46
Community empowerment strategies/ local constituency building, 55-73
  ATOD problems and, 55
  net effect of, 58
  planning of partnerships, 59-60

public/private sector coordination, 56
  outcomes of, 60-2
Community Exchange:
  definition and affiliation, 123
  goals and objectives, 126
  impact of, 128-130
  program design, 125
  public policy and, 130-6
  strategy, 127-8
  substance abuse reduction and, 127, 128
Community needs assessment,
  see Ethnographic research
Community Partnership Program, 58, 59, 64-5, 72
  coordination with other programs, 67-8
  evaluation, 65
  failed efforts of, 65-7
  funding, coordination, 69-70
  goal of, 64
Continental Congress, 1776, 11, 15
Contract with America, 35, 36
Criminal Justice System (CJS), 37
  violence prevention and, 41, 42

DARE Project, 24, 25, 134
Detoxification, 2
Drug Abuse:
  adolescents and, 21
  behaviors associated with, 3
  high-risk conditions associated with, 4
  prevention, 1-7
  relapse rates, 2-3
  violence, youth and, 33, 34, 35
  see ATOD abuse
Drug Free Schools and Communities Act (DFSCA), 22, 23-24

EPA, 14
Economic Development Act (1964), 63
Education:
  effectiveness/relevance of, 49
  failure of, 15
  health promotion strategies in, 51-3
  social justice, 12-13
  violence prevention and, 43, 44-5
Ethnographic research, xiv, 75-97
  building rapport, relationships, 83-4
  community needs assessment, purpose, 80-1
  data analysis, 87
  findings, 88-94
  instruments, 85-6
  interviewers, training, 86-7
  methods, 77-80
  multicultural social indicators, 80, 88-91
  procedures, 84-5
  process, 76-7
  sample, composition and selection, 81-3
  setting, 83
  systems change efforts, implications for, 94-6
  topics explored, 81
  validity and reliability, 87-8

Fighting Back, xi, xiv, 124, 147
  coordination with other programs, 67-8
  funding, 68
  mission statement, 99
  see Project Neighborhood (PNH)
Food and Drug Administration (FDA), 14
Ford Foundation, 67

Head Start, 147
Health and Human Services, 37, 64
Health for All Movement, 63
Health promotion strategies, xiii, 47-53
  adolescents and, 48-9
  cultural context of choice, 49-51
  mass media influence on adolescents, 50-51
  strategies, 51-3
Health, public, 11-2, 18, 19
  ATOD use and, 21
  inequality and, 59
  responsibility for, 62
  violence and, 37
Healthy People 2000, 63
Henry J. Kaiser Family Foundation, 68
Here's Looking at You, Two, 24
Hispanic Americans:
  drug-related crime reduction and, 65
  homicide rate, 39
  policy making, involvement in, 58
  poverty rate, xii
  urban population, xii
HIV-AIDS, 33, 35, 36, 48, 51
  community-based prevention, 58
  differentials between blacks and whites, 10
  local-constituency building, 71
  PNH, reported cases, 107

Join Together, xiv, 123-137
  goals, 125
  see Community exchange
Joint Center for Political and Economic Studies, xii
Just Say No, 50, 51, 53

192 Subject Index

Kaufmann Foundation, 144-5
Kerner Commission, xii

Methadone Anonymous (MA), 2
Midwestern Prevention Project, 61, 62
Milton S. Eisenhower Foundation, xii
Monitoring the Future study, 29
Mothers Against Drunk Driving (MADD), 63
Muslims, 43, 45

Narcotics Anonymous (NA), 2
National Cancer Institute, 6
National Institute on Drug Abuse (NIDA), 21, 61
National Partnership for a Healthy America, 72-3
National Research Council, 35
National Senior Survey, 1986, 21
Native Americans:
    policy making, involvement in, 58
    urban population, xii

Office for National Drug Control Policy, 67
Ottawa Charter for health promotion (Canada), 63

Partnership for a Drug-Free America, 124
Project Neighborhood (PNH):
    alcohol and drug indicators, 103-6
    alcohol public policy-covenants, xiv, 112-3
    ATOD problems, 100
    communicable disease indicators, 106-7
    community exchange, 135
    community mobilization models, xiv, 119-20
    community policing and crime rates, 120-1
    definition, xi
    faith community, prevention in (Project SAVE), xiv, 115-9
    goals, xiv
    mission statement, 100
    mortality indicators, general, 101-3
    outcomes, 112-21
    public awareness, xiv, 113-4
    systems change, impact on, 102
    target area description, 108-12
    theft/burglary rates, 107
    treatment indicators, 107-8
    treatment referral/tracking systems, xiv, 114
    see Substance abuse prevention resource systems
Project SAVE, xiv, 115-9
Promise Keepers, 43
Public Policy:
    alcohol, PNH and, 112-3
    community exchange and, xiv, 130-6

Racism, xiii, 15, 16
    endogenous institutions and, 15
    types, 9, 10
Relapse prevention, 2
    12-step programs, 3
    PNH and, 114
Robert Wood Johnson Foundation, xi, xiv, 68, 99, 115, 123, 147

School-based drug prevention programs, xiii, 21-31
    attitudes and use, 29
    clinical success, 29-31
    history, 21-4

intensity, 29
interactive programs, 25, 26, 29-30
meta-analysis, 24
non-interactive programs, 25, 26, 30
successful programs, elements of, 24, 30-1
unsuccessful programs, elements of, 25
what works/what doesn't work, 27-8
School Health Education Evaluation, 29
Social Inequity, indices, 9-11
Social Justice, 11-13
public health and, 18
Substance Abuse:
causes of, 17
crime and, 35
etiology, 7-8
poverty and, 35
risk factors for, 3-4
sexism and, 35
violence and crime, relationship to, xiii, 33-46
Substance abuse intervention, 1, 34
comprehensive program, requirements, 42-3
settings for, 4
Substance Abuse and Mental Health Services Administration, 64
Substance abuse prevention:
community strategy, 6
mass media and, 6-7, 50-1
outcomes, 5, 18, 29
paradigm for, 1-7
political climate and, 8
public awareness strategies, 5
social justice and, 11-3, 18
social/public policy, 6
targets for, 1, 2

see School-based drug prevention programs
Substance abuse prevention resource systems:
communities, 150
community exchange and, 136-7
guiding principles for, 148-50
operational functions, 152-3
prevention infrastructure, xv, 139-41, 151
prevention networks, xv, 141-2, 151
research and evaluation, xv, 143-5
systemic support, xv, 142-3, 151
Substance abuse prevention training system, 153-4
Substance abuse reduction, 127
Substance abuse treatment, 2-3
Surgeon General's Report to the Nation (1979), 62
Systems change:
definition, xii
Systems/organizations:
types, 13-19

Task Force on Alcohol and Drugs, 3
Three-strikes law, 39

United States Department of Education, 23
United States Department of Health, 62
Urban America:
racial composition, xii
violence in, 39

Violence:
child abuse and neglect, 38
commercial/business involvement in prevention, 45
community education, 42

domestic violence, 38, 43
firearms and, 38
gangs, youth and, 33-4, 35, 42, 46, 69
homicide rates, 37-8, 39
interpersonal violence, 39, 46
prevention, 34, 36, 42-5, 60
public health and, 37
rape, 38

substance abuse and, 33-46
suicide, 38

W.K. Kellogg Foundation, 68
Weber, Max, 13
World Health Assembly, 63
World Health Organization (WHO), 63

STUDIES IN HEALTH AND HUMAN SERVICES

1. Edward M. Bennett and Barry Trute (eds.), **Mental Health Information Systems: Problems and Prospects**
2. Thomas A. Shannon, **Twelve Problems in Health Care Ethics**
3. Barry Trute, Bruce Tefft, David Scuse, **Human Service Information Systems: How to Design and Implement Them**
4. Russell J. Sawa, **Family Dynamics for Physicians: Guidelines to Assessment and Treatment**
5. Edward M. Bennett and Bruce Tefft (eds.), **Theoretical and Empirical Advances in Community Mental Health**
6. Saul F. Rosenthal, **A Sociology of Chiropractic**
7. William S. Rowe and Sandra Savage, **Human Sexuality and the Developmentally Handicapped**
8. Erich H. Loewy, **Ethical Dilemmas in Modern Medicine: A Physician's Viewpoint**
9. Henry M. Butzel, **Genetics in the Courts**
10. Vincent J. Knapp, **Disease and Its Impact on Modern European History**
11. Edward M. Bennett (ed.), **Social Intervention: Theory and Practice**
12. Donald I. Warren, **Helping Networks of the Aging and Retired**
13. Margaret Rodway (ed.), **Counseling Diverse Client Groups: An International Perspective on Human Social Functioning**
14. Basil S. Georgopoulos and Luther Christman, **Effects of Clinical Nursing Specialization: A Controlled Organizational Experiment**
15. Joseph McMahon, **How to Select the Best Psychological Theory to be An Effective Counselor to Your Clients**
16. Pranab Chatterjee, **The Transferability of Social Technology: Explorations in the Knowledge Structures of the Helping Professions and Their Transfer**
17. Plinio Prioreschi, **A History of Human Responses to Death: Mythologies, Rituals, and Ethics**

18. Ursula Adler, **A Critical Study of the American Nursing Home - The Final Solution**
19. Margaret R. Rodway and Barry Trute (eds.), **The Ecological Perspective in Family-Centered Therapy**
20. Ursula Falk, **Interviews with Patients in Psychotherapy: The Client Speaks**
21. Theodora P. Dakin, **A History of Women's Contribution to World Health**
22. Dick Couey, **Nutrition for God's Temple**
23. Martha Brinton Mermier, **Coping with Severe Mental Illness: Families Speak Out**
24. C.A. Bartzokas, Emma E. Williams, and P.D. Slade, **A Psychological Approach to Hospital-Aquired Infections**
25. Coletta A. Klug, **Suicide: The Constructive/Destructive Self**
26. Jacob U. Gordon (editor), **A Systems Change Approach to Substance Abuse Prevention**